What Teens Are Saying About
12 Months of Faith:
A Devotional Journal for Teens . . .

"I lost my dad in a car a———— few months ago and have been struggling with my faith ———— ————n helping me get to the other side of ———— and feeling lost, I was really mad ———— I started going through this book. ———— on family, I was able to let go of my ———— od's hand comforting me. I also found tremendous com——— Scriptures provided after each question. This book was a turning point for me—so very important to working through my grief and reclaiming my faith—even deepening it."

William Shearron, 17

"This journal is the best one I've ever used because it's about dealing with real issues. As I read through the Bible passages, I discovered that I loved God far more deeply than I imagined, and now I really want to know God on a personal level. Read and work through this journal, and you'll see that it speaks to your heart. It's really awesome and loving. I recommend it to anyone who wants to know what they're up to in life."

Tara Russell, 14

"Working through *12 Months of Faith* is the best thing I've ever done for my own Christian growth. I've always enjoyed keeping a journal, but this one made me think about what's really important in my life. It answers questions that I've been unsure about and is leading me to ask questions I want to get more clear about."

Tony Bechan, 15

"This is one journal I know I will keep forever. Because of it, I've seen that I'm not alone in life; I'm not expected to know it all or go it alone. God wants us to walk with Him; He wants to be with us— and He will if we but let Him. After reading and working through this very personal journal, I no longer feel alone. God has never been more real to me than He is now. My whole youth group is going to use this for a devotional guide."

Sherre Feldman, 16

"My home life has not been very pleasant since my parents' divorce last year. My grandmother gave me this journal—and her timing couldn't have been more perfect. Now when things get confusing or painful, I go to my room, shut my door, get out my journal and my Bible and start in. I find comfort and meaning in the middle of the confusion. Those are the best moments of my day."

Connor Lane, 18

"Thank you for *12 Months of Faith*! This journal is giving me the wisdom and courage to look at life through different eyes. I've been struggling with smoking and drinking issues, primarily because so many of my friends are, so I guess I've been following along with the crowd. But this journal helped me understand just who I am: I'm a child, an 'heir,' of God—so I don't have to follow the crowd. I don't have to give in to peer pressure. The wisdom in this journal has been a most important anchor—a real lifeline."

Kelly Jolley, 17

"I never really understood what it meant to be 'born again' until I started going through this journal. I found it amazing that while I thought of myself as a Christian, I was just going through the motions, really. This journal taught me more about what the 'Christian walk' is than anything else I've read or been a part of."

Jose Garcia, 15

"Praying was always something I wanted to do, but I wasn't really sure if God would listen. After all, I haven't exactly been devoted to going to church or thanking Him for all the good things that have come my way in life. Then I started going through *12 Months of Faith*. Now I talk to God all the time, and I know He's listening, even when I've been less than perfect. This journal can really change your heart about the friendship God offers. And it will help you—for real—get a personal relationship with God. I hope you do. I did. And I can tell you that when you know God, you'll understand the real meaning of 'cool.' I know God now on a totally different level (or maybe it's that I know God for the first time—in a very real way)."

Brandon Keith, 17

12 Months of
FAITH

A Devotional Journal for Teens

Bettie B. Youngs, Ph.D., Ed.D.
Jennifer Leigh Youngs
Debbie Thurman
Bestselling authors of *A Teen's Guide to
Christian Living*

www.faithcombooks.com
www.tasteberriesforteens.com

Library of Congress Cataloging-in-Publication Data

Youngs, Bettie B.
    12 months of faith : a devotional journal for teens / Bettie B. Youngs, Jennifer Youngs, Debbie Thurman.
        p. cm.
    Includes bibliographical references (p.).
    ISBN 0-7573-0121-5
    1. Christian teenagers—Prayer books and devotions—English.
    2. Devotional calendars. I. Youngs, Jennifer Leigh, date.
    II. Thurman, Debbie. III. Title.

BV4850.Y67 2003
242'.63—dc21

                                                            2003051115

©2003 Bettie B. Youngs, Ph.D., Ed.D., Jennifer Leigh Youngs and Debbie Thurman
ISBN 0-7573-0121-5

Publisher: Faith Communications
            An Imprint of Health Communications, Inc.
            3201 S. W. 15th Street
            Deerfield Beach, FL 33442-8190

Cover design by Larissa Hise Henoch
Inside book design by Dawn Von Strolley Grove
Inside book formatting by Lawna Patterson Oldfield

To: _____

With Blessings!

From: _____

I have called you by name; you are Mine!

Isa. 43:1

Don't let anyone look down on you because you are young, but set an example in speech, in life, in love, in faith and in purity.

1 Tim. 4:11

Also by Bettie B. Youngs, Ph.D., Ed.D.

A Teen's Guide to Christian Living: Practical Answers to Tough Questions About God and Faith (Faith Communications)

365 Days of Taste-Berry Inspiration for Teens (Health Communications, Inc.)

A Teen's Guide to Living Drug-Free (Health Communications, Inc.)

A Taste-Berry Teen's Guide to Setting & Achieving Goals (Health Communications, Inc.)

Taste Berries for Teens #3: Inspirational Stories and Encouragement on Life, Love, Friends and the Face in the Mirror (Health Communications, Inc.)

A Taste-Berry Teen's Guide to Managing the Stress and Pressures of Life (Health Communications, Inc.)

More Taste Berries for Teens: A Second Collection of Inspirational Short Stories and Encouragement on Life, Love, Friendship and Tough Issues (Health Communications, Inc.)

Taste Berries for Teens Journal: My Thoughts on Life, Love and Making a Difference (Health Communications, Inc.)

Taste Berries for Teens: Inspirational Short Stories and Encouragement on Life, Love, Friendship and Tough Issues (Health Communications, Inc.)

Taste-Berry Tales: Stories to Lift the Spirit, Fill the Heart and Feed the Soul (Health Communications, Inc.)

A String of Pearls: Inspirational Stories Celebrating the Resiliency of the Human Spirit (Adams Media)

Gifts of the Heart: Stories That Celebrate Life's Defining Moments (Health Communications, Inc.)

Values from the Heartland (Health Communications, Inc.)

Stress & Your Child: Helping Kids Cope with the Strains & Pressures of Life (Random House)

Helping Your Child Succeed in School (Active Parenting)

Safeguarding Your Teenager from the Dragons of Life: A Parent's Guide to the Adolescent Years (Health Communications, Inc.)

Keeping Our Children Safe: A Guide to Emotional, Physical, Intellectual and Spiritual Wellness (John Knox/Westminster Press)

Getting Back Together: Repairing the Love in Your Life (Adams Media)

Also by Jennifer Leigh Youngs

A Teen's Guide to Christian Living: Practical Answers to Tough Questions About God and Faith (Faith Communications)

365 Days of Taste-Berry Inspiration for Teens (Health Communications, Inc.)

A Teen's Guide to Living Drug-Free (Health Communications, Inc.)

A Taste-Berry Teen's Guide to Setting & Achieving Goals (Health Communications, Inc.)

Taste Berries for Teens #3: Inspirational Stories and Encouragement on Life, Love, Friends and the Face in the Mirror (Health Communications, Inc.)

A Taste-Berry Teen's Guide to Managing the Stress and Pressures of Life (Health Communications, Inc.)

More Taste Berries for Teens: A Second Collection of Inspirational Short Stories and Encouragement on Life, Love, Friendship and Tough Issues (Health Communications, Inc.)

Taste Berries for Teens Journal: My Thoughts on Life, Love and Making a Difference (Health Communications, Inc.)

Taste Berries for Teens: Inspirational Short Stories and Encouragement on Life, Love, Friendship and Tough Issues (Health Communications, Inc.)

Feeling Great, Looking Hot & Loving Yourself! Health, Fitness and Beauty for Teens (Health Communications, Inc.)

Also by Debbie Thurman

A Teen's Guide to Christian Living: Practical Answers to Tough Questions About God and Faith (Faith Communications)

From Depression to Wholeness: The Anatomy of Healing (Cedar House Publishers)

Journaling from Depression to Wholeness: A 12-Week Program for Healing (Cedar House Publishers)

Hold My Heart: A Teen's Journal for Healing and Personal Growth (Cedar House Publishers)

Sheer Faith: A Teen's Journey to Godly Growth (Cedar House Publishers)

Contents

Acknowledgments

This book has been a divine journey and, as always, we'd like to thank those who have had a part in bringing it to our readers. First, to our publisher, Peter Vegso, whose publishing mission "to change the world one book at a time" has upped his ability to do just that. Faith Communications, the new Christian imprint making its home within Health Communications, will be speaking to our hearts and souls, thereby changing the world in the most "heavenly" ways! Thank you as well to the dedicated and talented staff at HCI, most especially those with whom we work most closely: Susan Tobias, Lisa Drucker, Christine Belleris, Lori Golden, Randee Feldman, Terry Burke, Kelly Maragni, Tom Sand, Larissa Henoch, Elisabeth Rinaldi, Kim Weiss and Brian Peluso—as well as to the many others who play an intricate role in transporting our words into the hands and hearts of our readers. As always, a special thanks to Andrea Perrine Brower, Anthony Clausi, Dawn Von Strolley Grove, Lawna Patterson Oldfield and all others involved in the mechanics of sending a book out into the world to work its magic.

From Bettie and Jennifer: During the course of this book, Everett (Bettie's father and Jennifer's grandfather), lost his six-month battle with melanoma. As we loved him through this trying time and watched his amazing courage as he began the task of what he called "looking candidly into the eye of death," we also witnessed the power of faith or, as he said, "God's love reaching out to me—and *for* me." Losing someone you love as dearly as we did this magnificent man puts all things into perspective. As we prayed with our "earthly father" to our Heavenly Father, we watched the grandeur of a human being ever so faithfully letting go of the people and things he loved in and about this world, and turn his full attention to his life beyond this realm. As his final days turned to final hours, it was with great peace and joy that he looked heavenward and said to us, "It's time for me to go home now, home to my Creator." As much as we feel "devastated" for our loss, we also feel the tranquility of our gain: Our dad/ grandfather is now with God. Such is the sole purpose of our earthly journey: *that we might know God.* So it is with special meaning and a great deal of gratitude that we bring you this book—and thankful that the writing of it came at this juncture in our own lives. We so firmly believe that this book can help you deepen your faith, and we pray that it will. We also would like to thank our dear friend, Debbie Thurman, and our many, many friends—and especially our many teen readers—for your love, support and prayers during this most poignant of times—a time when we witnessed firsthand one of God promises fulfilled, this time for our beloved dad and grandfather: "I have called you by name; You are mine" (Isa. 43:1).

From Debbie: Once again, I am deeply grateful for the privilege of working on a book that is another labor of godly love with Bettie and Jennifer Youngs. Thank you both from the well of my heart. God truly gave us a meeting of minds as we put this devotional journal together; it was His divine appointment, His providence, as was *A Teen's Guide to Christian Living.* I am grateful for the opportunity to have been steeped in God's grace as I went deep into His Word to discover in even more meaningful ways His awesome truths and "precious promises." We pass these along to the teens and others who will read this book. May they bless and grow you throughout your lives. Thank you to my husband, Russ, for his love, devotion and encouragement through our nearly twenty-two years of marriage. We are proof to anyone of any age that God answers prayer, and we delight in keeping Him at the center of our lives and our household. We are blessed to have two wonderful daughters, Jenni and Natalie, who are the apples of our eyes and who are rapidly growing into godly young women right before those eyes. The love of my family is the joy of my life, second only to my relationship with my Lord. I thank my mom and my grandmother as well, for their tireless cheerleading and the spiritual lessons they taught me from childhood. I also thank the many people who encouraged and lifted us up with their prayers through the writing and finalizing of this book. Thank you to the Genesis class at Thomas Road Baptist Church, and to my pastor, Jerry Falwell, who is always willing to contribute an uplifting word or gesture in support of my ministry.

God is faithful; His love endures forever. To God be the glory of this book.

Introduction

Have you ever asked questions such as, "Who am I?" "What is the purpose of my life?" "What am I supposed to do, and how will I know when I've discovered whatever it is I'm to be looking for?" "How do I understand my feelings—and survive all the ups and downs and in-betweens?" "How can I be as happy as I want to be, and have friends who like and admire me, without compromising my values or losing the 'me' in gaining the 'us'?" "How on Earth do I possibly make sense of all that is going on in the world and make a difference?" These are all awesomely complicated questions, and ones worth pondering, especially in the teen years. They are, after all, about understanding life—*your* life. Now that you're on the brink of adulthood, you naturally want to know who you're becoming, and where and how you fit in. You know it's time to stand up and be counted, time to look at life through your older and wiser eyes. It's time now to make a plan and set goals for yourself; it's time to make a difference in the world in which you're living.

Pursuing this great adventure takes much fortitude, doesn't it? Wouldn't it be great to have someone to help you, someone you could trust and count on to be your guardian, companion and best friend—and to know that this someone loved you more than life itself? You do: Your Heavenly Father has promised, "Have I not commanded you? Be strong and courageous. Do not be afraid, nor discouraged, for the Lord your

God will be with you wherever you go" (Josh. 1:9).

Do you believe that God is with you everywhere you go? He will be if you ask. He has promised, "Ask and it will be given to you; seek and you will find; knock and the door will be opened to you" (Matt. 7:7). God wants us to have an "up-close and personal" relationship with Him. In fact, knowing God is the very purpose of our lives. We're to grow our relationship with God every day. Studying God's Word and coming to Him daily in prayer help us to know Him as our Heavenly Father. And that's what *12 Months of Faith* is designed to do. This devotional journal can help you take your faith to another level: to develop a genuine fellowship with your Heavenly Father, and to see and know God as comforter, protector, guide, provider, teacher, friend, healer, shepherd and deliverer.

Make daily communication with God a habit. Some days we naturally will feel drawn to our Heavenly Father and will want to pour out our hearts to Him, either in thankfulness or in pain, depending on how our life is going at the time. On other days, it can be easy to crowd Him out in the busyness of our activities, or we can feel that things are going just fine without Him. Remember, *God desires special time alone with us, no matter what the circumstances of our lives.* Nothing should compete for our time alone with Him. *Make* time for God—*take* the time to know Him. Journaling is one of the best ways to do this. Reading, writing and studying God's Word can help you grow and fine-tune your relationship with Him.

In this devotional journal, we've chosen a particular theme for each month, reflecting twelve important areas of Christian growth. Each week's devotions explore a particular topic within this theme. This is followed by a question to help you gain an understanding of what it means to you and your life. Then we've provided Scripture so you may further study and reflect on the Word of God. We recommend that you memorize some of the daily verses so you will be able to recall them more easily, and find comfort and assurance during times of need. [Special note: We have provided you with forty-eight weeks of activities, but, as you know, there are actually fifty-two weeks in the year. Obviously, there will be extra days each month (except most Februarys) when there won't be a "week" to follow in the book. Use these extra days each month to reread or expand on sections you've already completed, especially those questions you may have skipped over because you weren't sure how you felt at the time and wanted more time to think things through. You might also use these extra days to reread certain Scriptures that are of particular interest to you and to think about their application to your life.]

In terms of beginning, feel free to start anywhere—just turn to a month that looks most interesting to you and begin. Each month stands alone, so it's not necessary to complete month #1 before you move on to month #2. Do your devotional study at a time when it's best for you. Many teens find that the last moments in the evening before bedtime are the best times for devotional reading or journaling. Others prefer to have private and alone time with God in the morning. And many teens find that, because devotions grow our personal relationship with God, they want to both open and close their days with this intimate time. However you choose to do it is up to you. The important thing is to make devotions a daily part of life. We invite you for the next week to spend ten minutes at the start of each day with the Lord. Looking over your question for the day, think on it and journal on it. Think of how you might make practical use of each lesson in your own life. Then take a few minutes to review the Scripture and make each verse a personal prayer. Ask God to make these truths a part of your life. Then thank Him for His faithfulness and goodness toward you. If you do this, you will find that, just as God causes the sun to rise every day—even when we can't see it—He is every bit as reliable at meeting your daily needs. If you have been fairly consistent in your daily times with God, you will begin to find that life looks different. What actually will have changed, however, is you and your outlook.

One important note: You may uncover some areas in your life that need some extra care and attention as you go through this journal. Perhaps you're concerned about a friend who is into drugs or how you can help her through the trauma of her parents' divorce. Maybe she's asked you to harbor a secret, and you're wondering what is the right thing to do—perhaps it is a very serious issue. Or you could be battling a problem such as an eating disorder, or an addiction to drugs, alcohol or even pornography. You may be dealing with the consequences of premarital sex, and maybe even a pregnancy. Perhaps you've been abused in some way—physically, emotionally or sexually. These are all serious problems that require serious, professional help. Please seek out a parent, school counselor, pastor or some trusted adult who can help you with these challenges.

God can give you insights and comfort if you lay these problems at His feet and ask for His help. He is our Counselor, our Great Physician and our Best Friend all rolled into one. Journaling along with prayer can help you to sort things out. Do you need to forgive someone—or yourself? God is into healing and forgiveness. It can be painful at first to look at these issues, but that pain won't last. It's just a door to healing. You will find much comfort and encouragement in this journal, along with some challenges to your thinking. It's all designed to help you see yourself as God sees you and to grow in His grace.

So take out your Bible and pen and begin. We recommend a student reference Bible in the New International Version (NIV) translation, if you don't already have one. Start now to discover who God is and who He wants you to be. Don't put it off. Begin the most important journey you will take—your walk with God for a lifetime. Turn to Him for guidance; praise Him as the source of miracles and blessings in your life; ask

Him to be with you every step of the way—in good times, bad times, all times.

In closing, we want you to know that you are dear to our hearts. We work with teens worldwide, and know of the hopes and fears you feel as you strive to live life with great heart. May you find comfort in asking God to walk with you every step you take. As always, we'd like to know how you found this book helpful and the ways it made a difference in your life—or to the friends or family members with whom you shared it.

You can visit our Web site at *www.tasteberriesforteens.com* or write us at:

Teen Team
3060 Racetrack View Drive
Del Mar, CA 92014

Blessings to you!
Bettie, Jennifer and Debbie

A SPECIAL WORD FROM THE AUTHORS

For the sake of simplicity and clarity, personal pronoun references to God in this book will be capitalized (i.e., He) while references to the person of Jesus Christ will be lowercased (i.e., he). This in no way makes a doctrinal statement, but serves to make clear the distinction between the two entities.

Month 1

COMMUNICATION: MEETING WITH GOD DAILY

God wants us to know Him. He wants a special and personal relationship with each of us. He wants us to seek His wisdom and instruction on a daily basis through prayer and reflection on His Word, the Bible. As we seek Him daily, He will help us to see more clearly and to know Him more completely. This is God's promise—that He will walk with us every moment of our lives. What an awesome knowing! Our Heavenly Father is always there, always ready to guide, guard, comfort and direct us, always ready to provide clarity when life gets complicated, painful and especially tough. Do you talk to our Heavenly Father on a daily basis?

QUESTIONS TO GUIDE THIS MONTH'S DEVOTIONS

- Is God *always* there for me?
- Is there a "best" way to talk to God—and how will I know when He's talking to me?
- Does God want to change everything about me?
- What signs can I look for that show me God is working in my life?

WeeK 1

Is God Always There for Me?

SCRIPTURE FOR REFLECTION

The Lord will keep you from all harm—He will watch over your life; the Lord will watch over your coming and going both now and forevermore.

Ps. 121:7–8

In this world of uncertainty, it is comforting to know that one thing remains constant: the love of God. The creator of the universe who always was and always will be is still the God of all comfort. He can intervene in the affairs of kings and nations one moment, and speak words of love and encouragement to us in His characteristic inner, quiet voice the next. God is totally awesome! He is everywhere at once. But what about all the pain, sorrow and suffering in the world—why would such a loving God allow it? God knows that every day brings the possibility of pain and hardship; after all, He gave us free will, and so we sometimes mess up, even hurt one another.

God has written His law on our hearts so that we might know how to live. He has given us His promises and "sealed" us for eternity with Him if we love Him and keep His commandments. In this, there is great hope and assurance. Yes, God is there for us 24/7. We can count on it. Can He count on us?

QUESTIONS TO THINK ABOUT
AND JOURNAL ON THIS WEEK

Have I questioned God's presence or love for me? If so, what
happened to make me doubt?

_____

_____

_____

_____

_____

_____

*Why are you troubled, and why do doubts arise
in your hearts? . . . It is I myself! Touch me and
see.*

Luke 24:38, 39

Do I do daily devotions or Bible reading? If so, what results do I
see? If not, am I willing to learn about faith and how it can be
more powerful in my life?

_____

_____

_____

_____

_____

_____

Your commands make me wiser than my ene-
mies, for they are ever with me. I have more
insight than all my teachers, for I meditate on
your statutes.

Ps. 119:98–99

Am I dealing with something confusing or painful at this moment?
What would I like to tell God about it?

_____

_____

_____

_____

_____

_____

_____

_____

O you who hear prayer, to you all men will
come. . . . Blessed are those you choose and
bring near to live in your courts!

Ps. 65: 2, 4a

Have I ever seen or experienced something I might call a *miracle*? If
so, what made me think it was God at work?

_____

_____

_____

_____

_____

Then the Lord said, "I am making a covenant with you. Before all your people I will do wonders never before done in any nation in all the world."

Exod. 34:10

Have I ever felt comforted when I cried out for help to God? How did that make me feel about Him?

_____

_____

_____

_____

_____

_____

_____

The Lord is my strength and my shield; my heart trusts in Him, and I am helped.

Ps. 28:7

Would I be willing to commit to just one month of daily devotions and prayer and see what God can do with that? What is the one thing I really want Him to do in my life during this month?

_____

_____

_____

_____

_____

_____

_____

*Do not be anxious about anything, but in every-
thing, by prayer and petition, with thanksgiving,
present your requests to God. And the peace of
God, which transcends all understanding, will
guard your hearts and your minds in Christ Jesus.*

                                        Phil. 4:6–7

Read Psalm 121. When the psalmist said, "The Lord will keep you
from all harm," did he mean that I would never have trouble if I trust
God or that God would bring me through difficult times? Why does
God allow me to experience pain and sorrow sometimes?

_____

_____

_____

_____

_____

_____

*I lift up my eyes to the hills—where does my
help come from? My help comes from the Lord,
the Maker of heaven and Earth.*

                                        Ps. 121:1–2

Week 2

Is There a "Best" Way to Talk to God, and How Do I Know When He's Talking to Me?

SCRIPTURE FOR REFLECTION

When you pray, go into your room, close the door and pray to your Father, who is unseen. Then your Father, who sees what is done in secret, will reward you.

Matt. 6:6

We can be assured that God can and does hear the sincere desires of our hearts, no matter how simple or urgent. "Before a word is on my tongue, you know it completely, O Lord," the psalmist tells us in Psalm 139:4. God communicates with us heart to heart.

We have little trouble going to Him with those 911 calls, but what about the day-to-day "God, what should I do about . . ." or "God, thank you so much for . . ." prayers? Are we too busy, or does the need to talk daily with God seem unimportant? Prayer has been called our "key by day and our lock at night." It should open and close all our days and be as natural as breathing. If Jesus came and sat down with us at mealtime or walked with us to school one day, we couldn't help but talk to him. We carry him with us always: His presence and his interest in our lives is real. If we listen patiently for that voice,

8

we'll "hear" it in the prick of our consciences, in the smile of our parents and grandparents; in the hug of a friend, or our own happy and peaceful hearts. Have you heard it lately? Has God heard *your* voice offering praise, thanksgiving, or asking for His love and guidance?

QUESTIONS TO THINK ABOUT
AND JOURNAL ON THIS WEEK

Have I been unsure of how to pray? If so, why? When was the last time I talked to God? (See prayers in Appendix A.)

The last time I actually talked to god one on one was at Kalahari, when I went with my church to a indoor water park. I was saved in the first session when I gave my life to Jesus. At that moment I could feel that I was with god, that I was with him and I could be with him.

Lord, teach us to pray.

Luke 11:1

Do I believe that God is just there in case of emergencies, or can I come to Him daily in prayer with whatever is on my mind? If I were to see God as my best friend, what would I say to Him right now?

I do not think god is just ther for emergencies because he loves us too much to let us feel bad all the time.

_____

_____

_____

_____

_____

Trust in the Lord with all your heart and lean not on your own understanding; in all your ways acknowledge Him, and He will direct your paths.

Prov. 3:5–6

Wouldn't my "best friend" want to hear about the good things in my life, too? What can I praise God for right now?

_____

_____

_____

_____

_____

_____

Delight yourself in the Lord, and He will give you the desires of your heart.

Ps. 37:4

What is one way that God might be trying to speak to me today?

_____

_____

_____

_____

_____

_____

_____

_____

*Here I am! I stand at the door and knock. If any-
one hears my voice and opens the door, I will
come in and eat with him, and he with me.*

Rev. 3:20

Do I try to live my life in the past or the future instead of moment by
moment? Jesus instructed us to ask God for our "daily bread" only.
Can I have that kind of relationship with God—one day at a time?

_____

_____

_____

_____

_____

_____

Who of you by worrying can add a single hour to his life? . . . Therefore, do not worry about tomorrow, for tomorrow will worry about itself.

Matt. 6:27, 34

Do I pray for others? Who do I know could use a special prayer right now? I offer it here to God:

_____

_____

_____

_____

_____

_____

Blessed are the poor in spirit for theirs is the kingdom of heaven. Blessed are those who mourn for they will be comforted.

Matt. 5:3–4

Jesus told us in his Sermon on the Mount to "seek first His kingdom," and God would take care of our daily needs. Is this difficult for me to accept? What am I trying to control? Can I handle it better than the God of the universe?

_____

_____

_____

_____

_____

For the pagans run after all these things, and your Heavenly Father knows that you need them. But seek first His kingdom and His righteousness, and all these things will be given to you as well.

Matt. 6:32–33

Week 3

Is God Watching Me All the Time?

SCRIPTURE FOR REFLECTION

I praise you because I am fearfully and wonderfully made. . . . When I was woven together in the depths of the Earth, your eyes saw my unformed body. All the days ordained for me were written in your book before one of them came to be.

Ps. 139:14, 15a–16

Do you sometimes think the world is so big and there are so many people that God couldn't possibly be worrying about *you* and caring about what you do with your life? God cares about each and every one of His children. Each of us is "fearfully and wonderfully made," each with our own set of unique gifts and our own identity. God speaks to each heart in the language it understands. God has a different purpose for you than He does for your neighbor. True, He wants us to honor Him in all we do and to gain collective strength from joining hands with other believers, all focused on worshipping and knowing the one everlasting and almighty God. He also asks us to submit our will to His will so that we can become even stronger and less likely to stumble and rebel in pride. But He expects you to be who you are—the unique person He made you to be.

14

No one could ever know you or love you like our Heavenly Father. The One who knew you in your mother's womb still knows you intimately and has His hand on your life. How will you honor Him with that life? If you were to stand before God and He were to say, "Why should I accept you into my heaven?" what would your answer be?

QUESTIONS TO THINK ABOUT
AND JOURNAL ON THIS WEEK

Do I consider myself to be a strong-willed person or more easygoing? How do I think this affects my relationship with God?

_____

_____

_____

_____

_____

_____

But as many as received Him, to them He gave the right to become children of God, even to those who believe in His name.

John 1:12–13 NASB

Have I thought about what my own unique gifts may be? Maybe I like to teach others or would rather comfort others. I believe that three special talents God has given me include (see Spiritual Gifts Survey in Appendix B):

- _____
  _____
- _____
  _____
- _____
  _____

> *But to each of us grace has been given as Christ apportioned it.*
>
> Eph. 4:7–8

What are some ways that I can use my gifts in service to God for the good of family, friends and community?

_____
_____
_____
_____
_____
_____
_____
_____

> *It was He who gave some to be apostles, some to be prophets, some to be evangelists and some to be pastors and teachers, to prepare God's people for works of service so that the body of Christ might be built up.*
>
> Eph. 4:11–12

Do I find that pride and stubborn self-will are sometimes problems for me? Do I need to do it my way instead of God's way? If so, how can I begin to change this?

_____

_____

_____

_____

_____

_____

_____

Do not love the world or anything in the world. For everything in the world—the cravings of sinful man, the lust of his eyes and the boasting of what he has and does—comes not from the Father but from the world.

1 John 15a–16

Have I ever prayed for God to make me more like Christ? If not, I can do it now. Here is my prayer:

_____

_____

_____

_____

_____

_____

_____

*Set your minds on things above, not on earthly
things. For you died and your life is now hidden
with Christ in God.*

Col. 3:2–3

Am I willing to let my friends influence who I am, but afraid to let
God guide me? How have I let friends or role models take away my
true identity?

_____

_____

_____

_____

_____

_____

*Blessed is the man who does not walk in the
counsel of the wicked or stand in the way of sinners or sit in the seat of mockers. But his delight
is in the law of the Lord, and on his law he meditates day and night.*

Ps. 1:1–2

Consider Psalm 139:7–10. Does it give me great comfort to realize
that God knows me that well—that His eye is on me all the time—
or does it make me uneasy? Why?

_____

_____

_____

_____

_____

_____

_____

Where can I go from your Spirit? Where can I flee from your presence? . . . O Lord, you have searched me and you know me. You know when I sit and when I rise; you perceive my thoughts from afar. You discern my going out and my lying down; you are familiar with all my ways. Before a word is on my tongue you know it completely, O Lord. You hem me in—behind and before; you have laid your hand upon me. Such knowledge is too wonderful for me, too lofty for me to attain.

Ps. 139:7; 1–6

Week 4

How Does God "Show Up" in My Life?

SCRIPTURE FOR REFLECTION

And we know that in all things God works for the good of those who love Him, who have been called according to His purpose. . . . What, then, shall we say in response to this? If God is for us, who can be against us? He who did not spare His own son, but gave him up for us all—how will He not also, along with him, graciously give us all things?

Rom. 8:28; 31–32

Do you believe that life just happens, or that God's purpose and power are behind everything? Are there really any coincidences? In the movie *Signs*, a priest who has faithfully served God turns his back on Him when his wife dies in a tragic accident. Yes, even men of God can fall victim to despair and doubt sometimes. The priest temporarily gave in to the false belief that we are on our own. But later, as he experienced what could only be divine intervention that saved the life of his son, his faith was restored.

Life can throw any of us into turmoil and doubt at times. If not for God's anchor to hold us steady through those storms, we would be left to depend on each other or ourselves. No human can be that strong. Inevitably, we will let each other down. Only God never fails. Do you trust God to be there for you, even when you can't see or feel His presence or nothing makes sense? There would be no need for faith if we could handle it all ourselves. Faith means holding on to God in the tough times that test our belief. If we seek Him daily and listen ever so closely with our hearts, He will make His will known in our lives. Are you willing to listen for His voice?

QUESTIONS TO THINK ABOUT AND JOURNAL ON THIS WEEK

When am I most reluctant to talk with God? Is it when things are going well and I think I don't need Him, or when trouble comes and I feel I can't find Him? Why?

_____

_____

_____

_____

_____

_____

_____

I know what it is to be in need, and I know what it is to have plenty. I have learned the secret of being content in any and every situation. . . . I can do everything through him who gives me strength.

Phil. 4:12–13

Have I experienced God's presence or help in my life in a way that left no doubt in my mind that it was Him? If so, what happened? If not, in what way do I need that kind of intervention right now?

_____

_____

_____

_____

_____

_____

_____

It was not by their sword that they won the land, nor did their arm bring them victory; it was your right hand, your arm, and the light of your face, for you loved them.

Ps. 44:3

Do I feel that God will only listen to me if I pray in a certain way? What does Romans 8:26–27 (see next page) mean to me?

_____

_____

_____

_____

_____

_____

_____

In the same way, the Spirit helps us in our weakness. We do not know what we ought to pray for, but the Spirit himself intercedes for us with groans that words cannot express. And he who searches our hearts knows the mind of the Spirit, because the Spirit intercedes for the saints in accordance with God's will.

Rom. 8:26–27

Am I willing to ask others to pray for me? Why or why not?

_____

_____

_____

_____

_____

_____

And pray in the Spirit at all times with all kinds of prayers and requests. With this in mind, be alert and always keep on praying for all the saints. Pray also for me.

Eph. 6:18–19a

Have I ever felt that God has let me down or refused to answer my prayer? If so, what did I learn from that time? Why do I think He doesn't always answer right away?

_____

_____

_____

_____

_____

_____

_____

_____

For the Lord your God is a merciful God; He will not abandon or destroy you or forget the covenant with your forefathers, which He confirmed to them by oath.

Deut. 4:31

What are some indications that God is working in a situation in my life right now?

_____

_____

_____

_____

_____

_____

_____

For it is God who works in you to will and to act according to His good purpose.

Phil. 2:13

Look at Romans 8:28 below. Is God more likely to change my circumstances or my attitude when I'm dealing with a problem? Which kind of intervention is likely to make me stronger?

_____

_____

_____

_____

_____

_____

_____

_____

And we know that in all things God works for the good of those who love Him, who have been called according to His purpose.

Rom. 8:28

Month 2

KNOWLEDGE: TAKING AN "UP-CLOSE AND PERSONAL" LOOK AT GOD AND HIS WORD

God continues to reveal Himself in many ways, both in the natural world and in our individual lives. His powerful creative force keeps the mysteries of the universe alive, while His compassion unites our spirits with His in love and service to others.

QUESTIONS TO GUIDE THIS MONTH'S DEVOTIONS

- Do I really know God? Do I have a relationship with Him?
- How well do I know God's Word? Can I apply it to my life?
- What is the purpose of each of God's three entities—the Father, the Son and the Holy Spirit?
- What does it really mean to be made "in God's image"?

Week 1

Who Is God?

SCRIPTURE FOR REFLECTION

The Lord reigns forever; He has established His throne for judgment. He will judge the world in righteousness; He will govern the people with justice.

Ps. 9:7–8

While it seems today that God has been reinvented to fit the designer image that various people want to assign Him, He is the same today as He *always was*. It's important to remember that He always was and always will be. We can't change God. He just *is,* period. "I AM" is how He referred to Himself when Moses wanted to know who was supernaturally talking with him thousands of years ago. "Oh," we can only imagine Moses saying in a small, scared voice.

Yet that same God who can make the Earth quake and the seas roar can also whisper His love to His people and alter circumstances for their benefit. He is both just and loving. He cares about our troubles and longs to spend time with us. All He asks is our devotion to Him and to each other with the same love. Can you accept that? God doesn't guarantee us an easy life, but He does promise to see us through life's ups and downs until our purpose on this Earth is fulfilled. There's no adventure more thrilling than walking with God by faith. Who is God to you? Are you really ready to know Him?

QUESTIONS TO THINK ABOUT
AND JOURNAL ON THIS WEEK

After reading Psalm 9, list some characteristics of God. Do I know God in all these ways?

_____

_____

_____

_____

_____

_____

_____

I will praise you, O Lord, with all my heart; I will tell of all your wonders.

Ps. 9:1

Is there something about God that confuses or frightens me? If so, what?

_____

_____

_____

_____

_____

_____

But they did not understand what this meant. It was hidden from them, so that they did not grasp it, and they were afraid to ask [Jesus] about it.

Luke 9:45

What about God is most comforting or reassuring to me?

_____

_____

_____

_____

_____

_____

_____

I, even I, am He who comforts you. Who are you that you fear mortal men, the sons of men, who are but grass, that you forget the Lord your Maker?

Isa. 51:12–13a

Does God seem fair to me? Why or why not?

_____

_____

_____

_____

_____

_____

_____

For I envied the arrogant when I saw the prosperity of the wicked . . . till I entered the sanctuary of God; then I understood their final destiny. Surely you place them on slippery ground.

Ps. 73:3, 17b–18a

How have I experienced God's patience or mercy in my life?

_____

_____

_____

_____

_____

_____

The Lord is not slow in keeping his promises. . . . He is patient with you, not wanting anyone to perish, but everyone to come to repentance.

2 Peter 3:9

How have I experienced God's discipline or correction in my life?

_____

_____

_____

_____

_____

_____

_____

Those whom I love I rebuke and discipline. So be earnest and repent.

Rev. 3:19

How have I experienced God's love in my life?

_____

_____

_____

_____

_____

_____

_____

_____

And so we know and rely on the love God has for us. God is love. Whoever lives in love lives in God, and God in him.

1 John 4:16

Week 2

What Are God's Promises to Me?

SCRIPTURE FOR REFLECTION

How sweet are your words to my taste, sweeter than honey to my mouth! I gain understanding from your precepts; therefore I hate every wrong path. Your Word is a light to my feet and light for my path.

Ps. 119:103–105

Psalm 119 is by far the longest Psalm in the Bible. It is a beautiful piece of Hebrew poetry in its original form. We can go to any section or stanza and read essentially the same celebration for God's Word. We may wonder why the psalmist chose to use such lengthy repetition, but when we stop to think of his overwhelming love of and respect for God's Word, we find ourselves getting caught up in that emotion with him. While he refers to God's Word as "the law" (the Jewish Torah) seven times, the psalmist also uses nine different synonyms for that divine law or teaching: testimonies, precepts, judgments, commandments, statutes, sayings, word, way and path. It's kind of hard to miss the point of this Psalm when its writer has so many ways of saying the same thing.

Is the Bible just a collection of old stories and obscure sayings for you? Have you ever read it with the purpose of knowing God better? The apostle Paul wrote to his young charge,

Timothy, "All Scripture is God-breathed and is useful for teaching, rebuking, correcting and training in righteousness" (2 Tim. 3:16). Are you willing to take a fresh look at God's Word and find out what He may be wanting to show you?

QUESTIONS TO THINK ABOUT AND JOURNAL ON THIS WEEK

With what parts of the Bible am I most familiar?

_____

_____

_____

_____

_____

_____

_____

I have hidden your word in my heart that I might not sin against you.

Ps. 119:11

Has a particular Scripture passage ever come to mind when I needed some comfort or godly counsel? What was it?

_____

_____

_____

_____

_____

_____

_____

_____

*Show me your ways, O Lord, teach me your
paths; guide me in your truth and teach me, for
you are God, my savior.*

Ps. 25:4–5

Do I accept the Bible as entirely God-inspired and true? Why?

_____

_____

_____

_____

_____

_____

_____

_____

*All Scripture is God-breathed and is useful for
teaching, rebuking, correcting and training in
righteousness.*

2 Tim. 3:16

In what ways do I think daily Bible reading or study could improve
my life?

_____

_____

_____

_____

_____

_____

_____

_____

Man does not live on bread alone, but on every word that comes from the mouth of God.

Matt. 4:4

Do I feel I need someone to help me interpret or better understand God's Word? Or do I believe that I can read on my own and pray for divine insight?

_____

_____

_____

_____

_____

_____

_____

I will instruct you and teach you in the way you should go. I will counsel you and watch over you.

Ps. 32:8

Do I believe the Word of God is relevant for me in today's times?

_____

_____

_____

_____

_____

_____

_____

_____

The Word of God is living and active. Sharper than any double-edged sword, it penetrates even to dividing soul and spirit, joints and marrow; it judges the thoughts and intents of the heart.

Heb. 4:12

Read Psalm 119:50–51 on the next page. How do those verses apply to my life? Can I name here at least one promise of God that I know?

_____

_____

_____

_____

_____

_____

_____

My comfort in my suffering is this: Your promise preserves my life. The arrogant mock me without restraint, but I do not turn from your law.

Ps. 119:50–51

Week 3

What Is the Holy Trinity?

SCRIPTURE FOR REFLECTION

But the Counselor, the Holy Spirit, whom the Father will send in my name, will teach you all things and will remind you of everything I have said to you.

John 14:26

Perhaps the most difficult thing to grasp about Christianity is the concept of a triune God—one God in three separate and distinct persons, or the Holy Trinity. We hear the phrase ". . . in the name of the Father, the Son and the Holy Spirit" without really understanding the significance of the Trinity. Although most of us understand God as the creator and sustainer of the universe, we are less likely to understand Jesus Christ as His human/divine son, our redeemer and the "Living Word." And what about the Holy Spirit? Who or what is that?

The ministry of Jesus' disciples began with the arrival of a supernatural power from on high to all believers. Jesus had told his disciples that after he ascended he would send back from heaven a "helper" who would give them power. That power was and is the Holy Spirit, the third person of the Trinity who searches the mind of God and intercedes for all believers. The anointing of the Holy Spirit enabled the disciples to convey the knowledge of God and the real meaning of Jesus' death and resurrection to those who had not heard this good news, even in languages they didn't previously know. In New Testament Greek, the Holy Spirit was called *Paracletos,* or one who comes alongside to instruct, comfort, convict and help. He is also the giver of spiritual gifts. If you have truly accepted Jesus as your savior, then the Holy Spirit lives in you. Have you felt your eyes being opened to some truth that you didn't understand before? Have you felt an unusual peace during a crisis? If so, you have known his presence.

QUESTIONS TO THINK ABOUT AND JOURNAL ON THIS WEEK

Have I found the concept or doctrine of the Holy Trinity confusing? In what ways?

_____

_____

_____

_____

_____

_____

_____

I, the Lord, have called you in righteousness; I will take hold of your hand. I will keep you and will make you to be a covenant for the people and a light for the Gentiles, to open eyes that are blind, to free captives from prison.

Isa. 42:6–7a

Is Jesus both Son of God and son of man to me? Do I accept his miraculous birth and his resurrection? Do I accept him as the "Living Word"? Why or why not?

_____

_____

_____

_____

_____

_____

_____

He who loves me will be loved by my Father, and I, too, will love him and show myself to him.

John 14:21b

Have I heard of the "fruit of the Spirit"? These are qualities that the Holy Spirit gives to us when we receive him. (See Gal. 5:22 on the next page.) Have I received the Spirit? If so, how do I demonstrate the fruit of the Spirit?

_____

_____

_____

_____

_____

_____

_____

But the fruit of the Spirit is love, joy, peace, patience, kindness, goodness, faithfulness, gentleness, and self-control.

Gal. 5:22

Why didn't Jesus give his disciples the Holy Spirit while he was still with them?

Maybe the disciples lacked the "fruit" of the spirit, love, Joy, peace, patience, kindness, goodness, faithfulness, gentleness, and self-control but then learned it when Jesus was no longer with him.

But I tell you the truth, it is for your good that I am going away. Unless I go away, the Counselor will not come to you; but if I go, I will send him to you.

John 16:7

Am I afraid people will call me a "Jesus freak" if I try to explain the power of the Holy Spirit to them? What is the best way for them to accept this awesome gift?

If you keep telling them about it and other people will help you tell them about it and show the bible to them they will hopefully accept it and follow Jesus.

> *God has raised this Jesus to life, and we are all witnesses of the fact. Exalted to the right hand of God, he has received from the Father the promised Holy Spirit and has poured out what you now see and hear.*
>
> Acts 2:32–33

If the Holy Spirit is my compass, then what (or who) is my map? How do I use both together?

The Holy spirit is the compass, so it leads you towards becoming a christian and believing in God, Jesus is The one who maps out all the things you will encounter throughout your life and together they will lead you to heaven.

> *In the beginning was the Word, and the Word was with God, and the Word was God. . . . In him was life, and that life was the light of men. The light shines in the darkness, but the darkness has not understood it.*
>
> John 1:1, 4–5

Read John 14:16–17, 26 and John 16:8–11. How many qualities of
the Holy Spirit can be found in these passages?

_____

_____

_____

_____

_____

_____

_____

_____

*I will ask the Father, and He will give you
another counselor to be with you forever—the
Spirit of Truth.*

John 14:16–17a

Week 4

How Am I Made in God's Image?

SCRIPTURE FOR REFLECTION

So God created man in His own image, in the image of God He created him; male and female He created them.

Gen. 1:27

What does it mean to be made in God's image? Who says we are made in His image, by the way? God in all three parts—Father, Son and Holy Spirit—declared that man would be made "in *our* image" at the dawn of creation (Gen. 1:26). Further in Genesis, after the Great Flood with which God destroyed all corrupt life on the Earth, requiring the faithful Noah's descendants to repopulate the Earth, God tells Noah that all human life is sacred because "in the image of God He made man" (Gen. 9:6).

What is the image of God in which we are made? How do we know what we are to be like? Well, we know from Scripture that God has certain distinct traits. He is jealous of other "gods" we may choose to worship (Exod. 20:5). He can be angry when we defy Him, although he is quite patient or "slow to anger." He is loving and compassionate. He is merciful and just in His dealings with us (Ps. 86:15). If we are made in God's image, it stands to reason that we are to have these same qualities. It's interesting to note that in 1 John 3:2 we are told we will be "like him," meaning Jesus, when we come into his presence in our own resurrected bodies one day. We are called "fellow heirs" to God's glory with Jesus Christ, another benefit of being made in God's image (Rom. 8:17). Furthermore, we are promised "the mind of Christ" here on Earth as we seek him in a personal relationship (1 Cor. 2:16). Have you considered how awesome it is to be so closely linked with the Creator of the universe?

QUESTIONS TO THINK ABOUT AND JOURNAL ON THIS WEEK

How do I see myself—as a miraculous creation of God or a product of chance? What does this say about my self-worth?

_____

_____

_____

_____

_____

_____

_____

For You created my inmost being; You knit me together in my mother's womb. I praise You because I am fearfully and wonderfully made.

Ps. 139:13–14

What does it mean to me to be an adopted son or daughter, a "fellow heir" with Christ?

_____

_____

_____

_____

_____

_____

For you did not receive a spirit that makes you a slave again to fear, but you received the Spirit of sonship. And by him we cry, "Abba, Father."

Rom. 8:15

Have I ever wondered why, if I am made in God's image, I am not perfect? How does our human weakness make our love for God and His for us more meaningful?

_____

_____

_____

_____

_____

_____

But God demonstrates His own love for us in this: While we were still sinners, Christ died for us.

Rom. 5:8

Do I believe God made any mistakes in His creation? If so, in what way?

_____

_____

_____

_____

_____

_____

_____

Oh, praise the greatness of our God! He is the Rock, His works are perfect, and all His ways are just.

Deut. 32:3b–4a

While all people are often called God's children, the word son (or daughter) is reserved in Scripture for those who have faith in Jesus Christ. If I am a Christian, these are my brothers and sisters in Christ. How does knowing this affect my attitude toward other Christians?

_____

_____

_____

_____

_____

_____

_____

You are all sons of God through faith in Christ Jesus.... There is neither Jew nor Greek, slave nor free, male nor female, for you are all one in Christ Jesus.

Gal. 3:26, 28

Can I see even those I dislike or who have hurt me as being God's children? Do I believe He loves us all equally? Why or why not?

_____

_____

_____

_____

_____

_____

_____

For God so loved the world that He gave His one and only Son, that whoever believes in him shall not perish but have eternal life. For God did not send His Son into the world to condemn the world, but to save the world through him.

John 3:16–17

Genesis 9 is an interesting book of the Bible. It contains a sacred covenant between God and man through Noah. Look at verses 4–6. What do these verses say to me about the value of life as created by God?

_____

_____

_____

_____

_____

_____

_____

_____

And for your lifeblood, I will surely demand an accounting. . . . For in the image of God has God made man.

Gen. 9:5a; 6b

Month 3

MAKING DECISIONS: ASKING GOD FOR GUIDANCE IN THE DECISIONS I FACE

God knows us better than we know ourselves. Although He doesn't promise us an easy life, He will lovingly guide our decisions and give us godly character as we overcome each challenge and obstacle with His help. He will never leave or forsake us—but He wants us also to make Him number one in our lives. Are you willing to ask God for His guidance in the decisions you make?

QUESTIONS TO GUIDE THIS MONTH'S DEVOTIONS

- How confident and bold does God want me to be in His presence?
- What is the most important aspect of friendship from God's viewpoint?
- How does God expect me to live my faith openly without being prideful?
- Does God care who my friends are, what career I will choose or who I date?

Week 1

Is God Watching the Choices I Make?

SCRIPTURE FOR REFLECTION

O Lord, You have searched me and You know me. . . . Before a word is on my tongue, you know it completely, O Lord. . . . For You created my inmost being. . . . I praise You because I am fearfully and wonderfully made.

Ps. 139:1, 4, 13, 14

Have you made any tough decisions lately? Maybe it's whether or not to remain friends with someone you're unsure of. Maybe it's not knowing what to do about a certain friend's party invitation where you know you'll have to confront choices you feel you're not ready to make. You could be toying with the idea of smoking or taking a drink with your friends. You may at times be tempted to take the easy way out and download a term paper from the Internet for a big class assignment—even knowing you may be found out. Maybe you're being pressured for sex by your boyfriend or girlfriend, and you're afraid you'll go too far. Maybe you're unsure how to tell a particular friend that you'd rather not hang around with him or her anymore. Maybe you're wondering how to attract into your life a certain special someone you'd like to get to know better. Maybe you're wondering how to be less up-front with your parents about social activities you'd like to be more a part of.

Every day in every way, we are faced with decisions. We can walk into these choices alone, or we can walk hand-in-hand with God, asking Him to guide our way. Our Heavenly Father cares about every decision that we have to make, no matter how big or small. God is there to comfort, guide and direct. Does it give you comfort or fear to think that your Heavenly Father knows all about you?

QUESTIONS TO THINK ABOUT AND JOURNAL ON THIS WEEK

Is God pleased with the choices I've made in my life so far? Why or why not?

_____

_____

_____

_____

_____

_____

In his heart a man plans his course, but the Lord determines his steps.

Prov. 16:9

Am I comfortable talking to my parents about decisions I must make? Why or why not?

_____

_____

_____

_____

_____

_____

_____

_____

Plans fail for lack of advisors, but with many advisors they succeed.

Prov. 15:22

Am I willing to let God direct me in the decisions I face?

_____

_____

_____

_____

_____

_____

_____

Two are better than one because they have a good return for their work.

Eccl. 4:9

What does Psalm 139:16 (see next page) mean to me? Does it mean I still have choices, even though God is in control?

_____

_____

_____

_____

_____

_____

_____

_____

> *All the days ordained for me were written in your book before one of them came to be.*
>
> Ps. 139:16

Am I afraid of the future, or do I face it with boldness and confidence?

_____

_____

_____

_____

_____

_____

_____

> *Do not fear, for I am with you; do not be dismayed, for I am your God.*
>
> Isa. 41:10

How am I willing to let God's Holy Spirit work through me?

_____

_____

_____
_____
_____
_____
_____
_____

*We do not know what we ought to pray for, but
the Spirit himself intercedes for us. . . . He who
searches our hearts knows the mind of the Spirit.*

Rom. 8:26, 27

In what ways am I being tempted right now? Am I considering
experimenting with drugs or alcohol? Do I need to be cool and
accepted by the "in" crowd? Will I ask God to guide me and give me
the courage to do what I know is right?

_____
_____
_____
_____
_____
_____

*Wine is a mocker and beer a brawler. Whoever
is led astray by them is not wise.*

Prov. 20:1

God is faithful; He will not let you be tempted beyond what you can bear. But when you are tempted, He will also provide a way out so that you can stand up under it.

1 Cor. 10:13

Week 2

Does God Care Who My Friends Are?

SCRIPTURE FOR REFLECTION

Blessed is the man who does not walk in the counsel of the wicked or stand in the way of sinners or sit in the seat of mockers. But his delight is in the law of the Lord, and on his law he meditates day and night. He is like a tree planted by streams of water, which yields its fruit in season and whose leaf does not wither.

Ps. 1:1–3

Our relationships with others are a reflection of who we are. Since we want our friends to have a positive influence on us (and we on them), how can we be sure about the character of our friends? Scripture gives us this guidance about the people with whom we associate: "Do not set foot on the path of the wicked or walk in the way of evil men" (Prov. 4:14). "Blessed is the man who does not walk in the counsel of the wicked or stand in the way of sinners" (Ps. 1:1). Look at the promise that follows in Psalm 1:3. "He is like a tree planted by streams of water. . . . Whatever he does prospers." Surrounding ourselves with friends who share our faith and outlook on life should be a habit we will want to cultivate for a lifetime. God's grace is never more evident than when He sends us a special friend or friends to walk with us and share both our joy and our pain. Do you have such a friend? Are you that kind of friend?

QUESTIONS TO THINK ABOUT AND JOURNAL ON THIS WEEK

Have I ever chosen the wrong friend? How did I know?

_____

_____

_____

_____

_____

_____

_____

He who walks with the wise grows wise, but a companion of fools suffers harm.

Prov. 13:20

How has a friend encouraged me or helped me through a difficult time?

_____

_____

_____

_____

_____

_____

_____

_____

A friend loves at all times.

Prov. 17:17

Has a friend ever led me down the wrong path? What happened? What did I learn?

_____

_____

_____

_____

_____

_____

_____

Do not be misled: "Bad company corrupts good character."

1 Cor. 15:33

Am I myself around my friends, or do I feel I need to be someone else?

_____

_____

_____

_____

_____

_____

_____

_____

> *Do your best to present yourself to God as one approved, a workman who does not need to be ashamed and who correctly handles the word of truth.*
>
> 2 Tim. 2:15

In what ways am I a good influence on my friends?

_____

_____

_____

_____

_____

_____

_____

> *Don't let anyone look down on you because you are young, but set an example for the believers in speech, in life, in love, in faith and in purity.*
>
> 1 Tim. 4:11

Do my friends share my faith? Does it matter to me that they do? Why or why not?

_____

_____

_____

_____

_____

_____

_____

_____

Make every effort to keep the unity of the Spirit through the bond of peace.

Eph. 4:3

Read Psalm 1:2 below. What do I think it means to "delight in the law of the Lord"?

_____

_____

_____

_____

_____

_____

_____

But his delight is in the law of the Lord, and on his law he meditates day and night.

Ps. 1:2

Week 3

Does God Care What Career I Will Choose?

SCRIPTURE FOR REFLECTION

Commit to the Lord whatever you do, and your plans will succeed. . . . When a man's ways are pleasing to the Lord, He makes even his enemies live at peace with him. Better a little with righteousness than much gain with injustice.

Prov. 16:3; 7–8

God made us, which means He knows us even better than we know ourselves. Surely, He must have the answer about what we are to do with our lives. Whether we're sure what we want to do, or completely clueless, it's reasonable to believe God know what's best and right for us. Yet, if we look around at the lives of other people, we see that God doesn't always roll out the red carpet to the ultimate choice right away. In times like this, we must remind ourselves that the way to choose best is to put the right amount of prayerful thought into it, to invite God to be a part of the process of deciding what is best and right for us.

Trust that God owns each life and each path. If a career choice looks attractive, but if it puts us in a position where we would have to, in any way, dishonor God, then we will know it's the wrong choice. Are you willing to ask God to reveal His plan for your life's work? Are you willing to ask God to guide and direct you, to open the right doors? Are you willing to follow God's guidance—to listen to His voice within?

QUESTIONS TO THINK ABOUT
AND JOURNAL ON THIS WEEK

What are two of my talents? In what way am I using these talents?

_____

_____

_____

_____

_____

_____

_____

But to each one of us grace was given according to the measure of Christ's gift.

Eph. 4:7 NASB

Have I been pleased with the priorities of my parents as they divide their time between family and career? What have they taught me?

_____

_____

_____

_____

_____

_____

_____

> *What good is it for a man to gain the whole world, and yet lose or forfeit his very self?*
>
> Luke 9:25

As I contemplate the job or career I will eventually pursue, what will be more important to me—the lifestyle it provides or the nature of my work?

_____

_____

_____

_____

_____

_____

_____

_____

> *Keep your lives free from the love of money and be content with what you have.*
>
> Heb. 13:5

What would I do if an employer asked me to do something illegal or immoral?

_____

_____

_____

_____

_____

_____

_____

_____

Fear the Lord and turn away from evil.

Prov. 3:7

If I felt God calling me to be a pastor or even a missionary, would I do it?

_____

_____

_____

_____

_____

_____

_____

It was he who gave some to be apostles, some to be prophets, some to be evangelists, and some to be pastors and teachers.

Eph. 4:11

How can I live my faith openly wherever I go? Am I doing this now? Why or why not?

_____

_____

_____

_____

_____

_____

_____

_____

Be diligent to present yourself to God as one approved, a workman who does not need to be ashamed and who correctly handles the word of truth.

2 Tim. 2:15

Read Proverbs 16:7 below. Do I believe this? Why or why not?

_____

_____

_____

_____

_____

_____

_____

When a man's ways are pleasing to the Lord, He makes even his enemies live at peace with him.

Prov. 16:7

Week 4

Does God Care Who I Date?

SCRIPTURES FOR REFLECTION

Above all else, guard your heart, for it is the wellspring of life.

Prov. 4:23

Be imitators of God, therefore, as dearly loved children, and live a life of love, just as Christ loved us and gave himself up for us as a fragrant offering and sacrifice to God. But among you there must not be even a hint of sexual immorality or of any kind of impurity.

Eph. 5:1–3

Do you long for that one perfect person—your only true love? Does that one person exist? Not really. It's a romantic notion. There are many people who are compatible enough with us to be our life's partner. We generally become interested in a number of people before finding the one we want to marry. It's okay just to have fun hanging out with different people along the way and not to see everyone we date as a potential life partner. Dating helps us to get to know someone and to figure out what we really desire in the person we eventually will marry. But we don't have to figure this out alone: God's rule is to be "equally yoked." That means when we're ready, we should look for a person who shares our faith above all, but also some of our interests and dreams. Love is meant to grow and mature. The idea is to grow more together instead of apart.

Do you struggle with what is proper in a serious dating relationship and what is not? The desire for sexual intimacy is a natural part of our God-given makeup as we mature, but the act of sex is meant only for marriage. Therefore, we need to establish boundaries for intimacy in our relationships. Can you resist sexual pressures from your friends or the person you are dating? You can with God's help.

QUESTIONS TO THINK ABOUT
AND JOURNAL ON THIS WEEK

Am I comfortable with friends of the opposite sex, or do I feel I don't measure up? How does God want me to see myself?

_____

_____

_____

_____

_____

_____

_____

There is a time for everything and a season for every activity under the sun. . . . He has made everything beautiful in its time.

Eccl. 3:1; 11

What qualities must someone have before I consider that person some-one I'd like to date? How will I know if that person is my "soul mate"?

_____
_____
_____
_____
_____
_____
_____
_____

Place me like a seal over your heart, like a seal on your arm; for love is as strong as death.

Song of Solomon 8:6

Have I gone too far in physical intimacy with a boyfriend or girl-friend? What does it mean to be a "secondary virgin"?

_____
_____
_____
_____
_____
_____

If we confess our sins, he is faithful and just and will forgive us our sins and purify us from all unrighteousness.

1 John 1:9

Do I believe that virginity is just a nice, antiquated idea whose time has come and gone? Is it too hard to save myself for marriage? Why or why not?

_____

_____

_____

_____

_____

_____

> *Marriage should be honored by all, and the marriage bed kept pure, for God will judge the adulterer and all the sexually immoral.*
>
> Heb. 13:4

Do I believe that marriage is for keeps or just as long as two people stay in love?

_____

_____

_____

_____

_____

_____

Love is patient, love is kind. . . . It always pro-
tects, always trusts, always hopes, always perse-
veres. Love never fails.

1 Cor. 13:4, 7, 8a

What if God's purpose is for me to remain single? Could I accept
that? Why or why not?

_____

_____

_____

_____

_____

_____

_____

I wish that all men were as I am [unmarried]. But
each man has his own gift from God; one has this
gift, another has that.

1 Cor. 7:7

Why do I believe many marriages end in divorce?

_____

_____

_____

_____

_____

_____

_____

*[Love] does not envy, it does not boast, it is not
proud. It is not rude, it is not self-seeking, it is not
easily angered, it keeps no records of wrongs.*

1 Cor. 13:4b–5

Read Ephesians 4:22–24 below. How does the teaching of Jesus
(and the apostle Paul here) give me confidence to respect my friends
and dating partners?

_____

_____

_____

_____

_____

_____

_____

*You were taught, with regard to your former way
of life, to put off your old self, which is being
corrupted by its deceitful desires; to be made new
in the attitude of your minds; and to put on the
new self, created to be like God in righteousness
and holiness.*

Eph. 4:22–24

Month 4

"DISCERNMENT": KNOWING THE DIFFERENCE BETWEEN TRUTH AND LIES

With all the influences in the world, it is easy to be led astray. God, however, gives us the ability through His Word and the presence of the Holy Spirit to tell the difference between what *appears* to be true and upright and what actually is true. Then He gives us the courage to act on that knowledge.

QUESTIONS TO GUIDE THIS MONTH'S DEVOTIONS

- Do I understand what truth really is, or am I led astray?
- How will I be able to stand firm against the real enemy of my soul?
- What is sin? Can I avoid it?
- How can I tell the difference between what appears good and what actually is best?

Week 1

How Can God's Truth Keep Me from Being Led Astray?

SCRIPTURE FOR REFLECTION

In the beginning was the Word and the Word was with God and the Word was God. . . . In him was life, and that life was the light of men. . . . I am the light of the world. Whoever follows me will never walk in darkness, but will have the light of life.

John 1:1, 4; 8:12

What does the concept of *truth* mean to you? Regardless of how some people would like to base truth on their own beliefs and convictions, there is only one author of truth: God. And He hasn't changed the definition since He set it forth.

God *is* truth and light. His son Jesus was the embodiment of that truth when he lived among us on Earth. "I am the way and the truth and the life," he said in John 14:6, adding that if we know him, we also know the Father. Jesus is the Living Word that reveals God's truth. When we come to know him, we can see more clearly.

After Jesus came to Earth, suffered death for our sins and returned back to his heavenly home, he sent the Holy Spirit as a counselor and helper to each believer. Through the Spirit, we receive instruction about what is real and what is not. Through the Spirit, our eyes are opened to the truth of the Scriptures as we read. John 1:5 tells us, "The light shines in the darkness, but the darkness has not understood it." Those who choose to live on their own will stumble in the darkness, never understanding the power of God's truth. Where are you today in your journey? Are you in the shadows still, or are you coming into the light?

QUESTIONS TO THINK ABOUT AND JOURNAL ON THIS WEEK

Before reading today's devotional thought and Scripture, what was my idea of truth? What is it now?

_____

_____

_____

_____

_____

_____

_____

_____

_____

_____

The man without the Spirit does not accept the things that come from the Spirit of God, for they are foolishness to him, and he cannot understand them, because they are spiritually discerned.

1 Cor. 2:14

Have I seen God's truth at work in my life? If so, in what ways?

_____

_____

_____

_____

_____

_____

_____

_____

Instead, speaking the truth in love, we will in all things grow up into him who is the Head, that is, Christ.

Eph. 4:15

Why can't truth be relative or based on my own needs and beliefs?

_____

_____

_____

_____

_____

_____

_____

But if you harbor bitter envy and selfish ambition in your hearts, do not boast about it or deny the truth. Such "wisdom" does not come down from heaven, but is earthly, unspiritual, of the devil.

James 3:14–15

If I'm not living according to God's truth, am I automatically living according to a lie? Why or why not?

_____

_____

_____

_____

_____

_____

_____

> *This is the message we have heard from him and declare to you: God is light; in Him there is no darkness at all. If we claim to have fellowship with Him, yet walk in the darkness, we lie and do not live by the truth.*
>
> 1 John 1:5–6

Do I believe that Jesus Christ is "the way and the truth and the life"? What does this mean to me?

_____

_____

_____

_____

_____

_____

_____

Even the demons believe that—and shudder.

James 2:19

Have I experienced the negative power of living under a lie? How did I come to know it was a lie?

_____

_____

_____

_____

_____

_____

_____

I am the good shepherd. The good shepherd lays down his life for the sheep. The hired hand is not the shepherd who owns the sheep. So when he sees the wolf coming, he abandons the sheep and runs away. Then the wolf attacks the flock and scatters it.

John 10:11–12

Look at John 8:32 again on the next page. What did Jesus mean when he said "the truth will set you free"?

_____

_____

_____

_____

_____

_____

_____

If you hold to my teaching, you are really my disciples. Then you will know the truth, and the truth will set you free.

John 8:32

Week 2

Is Satan Real?

SCRIPTURE FOR REFLECTION

Put on the full armor of God so that you can take your stand against the devil's schemes. For our struggle is not against flesh and blood, but against the rulers, against the authorities, against the spiritual forces of evil in the heavenly realms.

Eph. 6:11–12

In order for the truth to become evident, it must be seen in contrast to its opposite. Lies are the language of our enemy, Satan. He is the "father of lies," the prince of darkness and deception, the "thief who comes to steal and kill and destroy" (John 10:10). Oh, he's real all right. His power is in his ability to deceive and to appear as an "angel of light" (2 Cor. 11:14). Can we help it if we are so deceived? It's not as if the enemy comes to us with horns, a tail and a pitchfork. Yet, God expects us to know His truth and to avoid that deception. He gives us a way of escape from the schemes of the evil one.

Even though Satan is no match for God, he can do great damage in our lives and cause great pain. While we must feel the consequences of our mistakes, even if we are deceived into making them, we have the promise of forgiveness and redemption through Jesus, the light and salvation of the world. Do you know this? Are you comforted by the promise that "the one who is in [me] is greater than the one who is in the world" (1 John 4:4)?

QUESTIONS TO THINK ABOUT
AND JOURNAL ON THIS WEEK

Have I been unwilling to accept Satan as a real spiritual enemy in my life? If so, how will I reconsider that now?

_____

_____

_____

_____

_____

_____

Be self-controlled and alert. Your enemy the devil prowls around like a roaring lion looking for someone to devour.

1 Peter 5:8

When is the most recent time I felt I was being tempted to do something I knew was wrong? What was going on? Who won?

_____

_____

_____

_____

_____

_____

_____

Resist him, standing firm in the faith, because you know that your brothers throughout the world are undergoing the same kind of sufferings.

1 Peter 5:9

Have I asked for God's protection and guidance in my life lately? In what way do I need some direction right now?

_____

_____

_____

_____

_____

_____

_____

Ask and it will be given to you; seek and you will find; knock and the door will be opened to you.

Matt. 7:7

What does it mean to "put on the armor of God"? What is the one piece of armor I need the most today?

_____

_____

_____

_____

_____

_____

_____

> *Therefore put on the full armor of God, so that when the day of evil comes, you may be able to stand your ground, and after you have done everything, to stand.*
>
> Eph. 6:13

Have I ever done something I knew was wrong just to gain the approval of some friends? What was it? Are those friends still my friends? Why or why not?

_____

_____

_____

_____

_____

_____

> *For they loved praise from men more than praise from God.*
>
> John 12:43

If I knew that a friend was about to make a big mistake, would I be willing to confront that person with the truth in love? What could I do or say that might make a difference? How would I feel if that person ignored or mocked me?

_____

_____

_____

_____

_____

_____

_____

_____

A servant of the Lord must not quarrel, but must gently instruct, in the hope that God will grant them repentance leading them to a knowledge of the truth.

2 Tim. 2:25

Look at Ephesians 6:18 below. How does this instruction compare with the duties of a soldier who is on guard duty?

_____

_____

_____

_____

_____

_____

_____

And pray in the Spirit on all occasions with all kinds of prayers and requests. With this in mind, be alert and always keep on praying for all the saints.

Eph. 6:18

Week 3

What Is Sin?

SCRIPTURE FOR REFLECTION

Everyone who sins breaks the law; in fact, sin is lawlessness. But you know that he appeared so that he [Jesus] might take away our sins. And in him, there is no sin.

1 John 3:4–5

Sin is not a new word to us, but neither is it one we use comfortably. Do we really know what sin is? We might say it is breaking any of the Ten Commandments, or what we know as God's law. That's pretty obvious. What about those troublesome, gray areas of life where it's not quite so clear to us what the right action should be? Can we cheat just a little if the test is going to be impossibly hard? Can we take some office supplies from our parents' workplace because they're convenient? Can we lie about something if we think it's justified by the results? Can we get physically intimate with a boyfriend or girlfriend if we really love each other?

We're all going to make mistakes in this life because "all have sinned and fall short of the glory of God" (Rom. 3:23). But that's not the end of the story. Our hope of redemption is in Christ. Had God not sent His son to take our place and be punished for our sins, once for all time, we would be hopelessly lost. God convicts us or reveals the sin in our lives. Satan accuses or imprisons us with false guilt. Do you know the difference? You will if you keep believing in the one who came to set you free—Jesus Christ.

QUESTIONS TO THINK ABOUT
AND JOURNAL ON THIS WEEK

Have I looked at sin more as a deliberate act of rebellion against God or as the act of being deceived? How responsible am I for my sins?

_____

_____

_____

_____

_____

_____

_____

_____

Remember not the sins of my youth and my rebellious ways. According to your love remember me.

Ps. 25:7

Do I feel unusually guilty about things I've done or just about myself in general? If so, am I willing to talk to God about things?

_____

_____

_____

_____

_____

_____

_____

Therefore there is now no condemnation for those who are in Christ Jesus, because through Christ Jesus the law of the Spirit of Life set me free from the law of sin and death.

Rom. 8:1–2

Am I at the other end of the scale, having little or no sense of conscience or conviction about sin in my life? In what way is that dangerous and destructive?

_____

_____

_____

_____

_____

_____

_____

Therefore do not be foolish, but understand what the Lord's will is.

Eph. 5:17

Do I sometimes feel it's impossible to escape sin's power in my life? If so, what truth have I learned this month that can change that for me?

_____

_____

_____

_____

_____

_____

_____

_____

> *So I find this law at work: When I want to do good, evil is right there with me. For in my inner being, I delight in God's law; but I see another law at work in the members of my body.*
>
> Rom. 7:21–23a

Does it give me comfort to know that even Jesus was tempted by Satan? Why or why not?

_____

_____

_____

_____

_____

_____

_____

_____

> *Away from me, Satan! For it is written: "Worship the Lord your God and serve Him only."*
>
> Matt. 4:10

Was there a time I succeeded in overcoming a particular temptation? If so, how did I do it? Do I believe God will always provide an "escape" for me?

_____

_____

_____

_____

_____

_____

_____

*No temptation has seized you except what is
common to man; and God is faithful; He will not
let you be tempted beyond what you can bear.
But when you are tempted, He will also provide
a way out so that you can stand up under it.*

1 Cor. 10:13

Read 1 John 3:13. Have I experienced someone ridiculing me
because of my faith? If so, how do I handle it in a way that is pleasing to God?

_____

_____

_____

_____

_____

_____

*But in your hearts, set apart Christ as Lord.
Always be prepared to give an answer to everyone who asks you to give the reason for the hope
that you have. But do this with gentleness and
respect, keeping a clear conscience, so that those
who speak maliciously against your good behav-
ior in Christ may be ashamed of their slander.*

1 Peter 3:15–16

Week 4

How Do I Know if I'm Being Deceived?

SCRIPTURE FOR REFLECTION

The wicked boasts of his heart's desire. . . . All his thoughts are, "There is no God." . . . He lurks in a hiding place as a lion in his lair; he lurks to catch the afflicted.

Ps. 10:3a, 4b, 9 NASB

While Psalm 10 speaks of people who do evil, it also describes the tactics of Satan himself, who has deceived these people and seeks to do the same to us. Not only do the deceived believe there is no God, but they cannot see the one who holds the cover over their eyes. It's a pretty sad place to be. These poor, blind folks lead others into the same blindness. Have you been led off in the wrong direction by one of Satan's followers? Chances are, you never even knew it. There is a way to see through this deception, however. Keeping the truth of the Word—the "light for my path"—before us is the one sure way to break the spell of the evil one. He's tough, but he's not invincible.

Every day, we face the challenge of keeping ourselves pure and bathed in the light of the truth. We may trip and fall now and then, but we don't need to stay down. We simply get up, dust ourselves off and pick up the journey where we left off. Every victory for us is a defeat for the father of lies.

QUESTIONS TO THINK ABOUT
AND JOURNAL ON THIS WEEK

Why does Satan have to use trickery to get us to do his will?

_____

_____

_____

_____

_____

_____

_____

_____

*Resist the devil and he will flee from you. Come
near to God and he will come near to you.*
James 4:7–8

In what ways am I better able to understand the subtle dangers of
the enemy now?

_____

_____

_____

_____

_____

_____

_____

_____

Simon, Simon, Satan has asked permission to sift you as wheat. But I have prayed for you, Simon, that your faith may not fail.

Luke 22:31–32

Of all the defenses available to me, which has been the most effective in helping me to avoid Satan's deception? Is it prayer? Reading God's Word? Being accountable to someone who is more spiritually mature than me?

_____

_____

_____

_____

_____

_____

_____

Even though I walk through the valley of the shadow of death, I will fear no evil, for You are with me.

Ps. 23:4

Have I ever been able to see a trap that someone else was about to fall into, even when that person couldn't? If so, why do I think I could see when he or she couldn't?

_____

_____

_____

_____

_____

_____

_____

_____

The way of a fool seems right to him, but a wise man listens to advice.

Prov. 12:15

Is there an area in my life where I am especially weak or vulnerable to spiritual attack by the enemy? What is it? Does he always seem to attack me there?

_____

_____

_____

_____

_____

_____

_____

Watch and pray so that you will not fall into temptation. The spirit is willing, but the body is weak.

Matt. 26:41

What do I see as my area of strength where I am not likely to get attacked?

_____

_____

_____

_____

_____

_____

_____

_____

*Be on your guard; stand firm in the faith; be men
[and women] of courage; be strong.*

1 Cor. 16:13

Looking at Psalm 10, in what ways does the psalmist describe the
ignorance and doom of the wicked who won't repent?

_____

_____

_____

_____

_____

_____

_____

*Why does the wicked man revile God? Why
does he say to himself, "He won't call me to
account?"*

Ps. 10:13

Month 5

TRUST:
RELYING ON GOD 24/7

God is in charge of the universe and all that happens in it, even when it appears that things are out of control. What a great comfort: We can trust there is a divine purpose for everything under the sun. God wants only the best for His children.

QUESTIONS TO GUIDE
THIS MONTH'S DEVOTIONS

- How can I be sure that God has everything under control?
- Why must bad things sometimes happen, even to godly people?
- How has fear affected my life, and how can God overcome it?
- Why doesn't God guarantee Christians an easy life?

Week 1

Is God Always on Duty— Everywhere?

SCRIPTURE FOR REFLECTION

God is our refuge and strength, an ever-present help in trouble. . . . Be still and know that I am God.

Ps. 46:1, 10a

The world is an uncertain place, full of wars and bullies and disasters of every kind. Peace seems so far off as to be impossible. "Where is God?" we wonder in these difficult times. God is in the same place He has been in all the difficult times of ages past. Just as God tells us He will set a banquet table for us in "the presence of my enemies" (Ps. 23:5), He reminds us that we must "be still" and know who He is. That's not easy, is it? Even so, if we couldn't believe that God really is on duty, ever watchful and ready to intervene if He so chooses, life truly would be unbearable. Sometimes, He refuses to help us *out* of a situation because He knows we will gain strength and more trust in Him by bearing up under the weight and allowing Him to see us *through* the challenge instead.

We have the assurance of the Holy Spirit as our comforter and encourager, a most amazing gift. Jesus asks us to come to him and to let him carry our burdens with us. Like two horses or oxen that are yoked together so they may pull much more than twice their individual share of the weight, Jesus walks beside us, helping to share the load and greatly multiply our strength. Are you allowing the Savior to help you in this way, or are you trying to carry the whole load yourself?

QUESTIONS TO THINK ABOUT
AND JOURNAL ON THIS WEEK

Have I doubted God's presence in my life lately? Where do I feel He is right now?

_____

_____

_____

_____

_____

_____

_____

> He said to them, "Why are you troubled, and why do doubts rise in your minds? Look at my hands and my feet. It is I myself!"
>
> Luke 24:38–39a

Was there a time when God gave me strength to make it through a challenge I couldn't face on my own? What happened?

_____

_____

_____

_____

_____

_____

_____

_____

*He gives strength to the weary and increases the
power of the weak.*

                                    Isa. 40:29

Has there been a troubling time in my life when I prayed and just
couldn't seem to find God? How did that situation end up? What
did I learn?

_____

_____

_____

_____

_____

_____

_____

*I say to God my Rock, "Why have you forgotten
me?". . . Put your hope in God, for I will yet
praise Him, my Savior and my God.*

                                    Ps. 42:9a; 11b

Am I frightened by the current world unrest, especially the war on terror? How can I see God working in all that?

_____

_____

_____

_____

_____

_____

You will hear of wars and rumors of wars, but see to it that you are not alarmed. Such things must happen, but the end is still to come.

Matt. 24:6

Do I pray for the world's leaders? Or do I feel that my little prayers are so insignificant that God won't hear them?

_____

_____

_____

_____

_____

_____

By me kings reign, and rulers make laws that are just; by me princes govern, and all nobles who rule on Earth.

Prov. 8:15–16

Have I asked God to intervene in a situation closer to home, like a family dispute or a problem at school? If so, how do I see Him working in that?

_____

_____

_____

_____

_____

_____

_____

It is God who works in you to will and to act according to His good purpose.

Phil. 2:13

"Be still" is also translated as "cease striving." Why does God want me to cease striving, or trying on my own, and know that He is my God? Does that mean He wants me to do nothing?

_____

_____

_____

_____

_____

_____

_____

_____

"Be still, and know that I am God" . . . *The Lord God Almighty is with us; the God of Jacob is our fortress.*

Ps. 46:10a; 11

WeeK 2

Why Does God Let Bad Things Happen to Good People?

SCRIPTURE FOR REFLECTION

*All was well with me, but He shattered me. . . .
My face is red with weeping, deep shadows ring
my eyes; yet my hands have been free of violence
and my prayer is pure.*

Job 16:12a; 16–17

The book of Job has been the age-old example of how to persevere in the face of extreme and undeserved adversity. Although Job was "blameless and upright," God allowed Satan to take virtually everything from him, including his health, his children and his wealth. God's only restriction on Satan was to prohibit him from taking Job's life. Satan wanted Job to turn away from God, but Job did not, even though he cried out angrily to God in his pain and anguish. God came to Job and helped him to understand what was happening. Job humbled himself before God and repented of his anger, and God restored him to health and even more prosperity than before. God will find a way to help you believe, even if it means allowing you to know pain and hardship first. Without the storm, there can be no rainbow.

QUESTIONS TO THINK ABOUT
AND JOURNAL ON THIS WEEK

Does it seem to me that things just happen arbitrarily, with no rhyme or reason? Or can I accept that God is in everything, even when it's painful?

_____

_____

_____

_____

_____

_____

God will bring to judgment both the righteous and the wicked, for there will be a time for every activity, a time for every deed.

Eccl. 3:17

Have I been allowed to experience a tragedy that appeared meaningless? If so, where am I in my journey to understand it—still struggling or beginning to see God's purpose?

_____

_____

_____

_____

_____

_____

_____

I tell you the truth, you will weep and mourn while the world rejoices. You will grieve, but your grief will turn to joy.

John 16:20

Have I known a good person who lost his or her faith because of some tragedy or hardship? What would I say to comfort that person if I had the chance? Would I know how?

_____

_____

_____

_____

_____

_____

_____

Do not be afraid of what you are about to suffer. . . . Be faithful, even to the point of death, and I will give you the crown of life.

Rev. 2:10

How would I want to be comforted by someone if I were struggling with my faith?

_____

_____

_____

_____

_____

_____

_____

_____

And Saul's son Jonathan went to David at Horesh and helped him find strength in God. "Don't be afraid," he said. . . . The two of them made a covenant before the Lord.

1 Sam. 23:16–17a; 18a

Does God allow me to express my anger or frustration to Him, to a point? How far can I go without sinning against Him?

_____

_____

_____

_____

_____

_____

_____

Then Elihu said, "Do you think this is just? You say, 'I will be cleared by God.' Yet you ask Him, 'What profit is it to me, and what do I gain by not sinning?' "

Job 35:1–3

Job's friends—particularly the younger Elihu—spoke some truth to him, but they also gave some empty advice and criticism. Have I ever had a friend or friends try to give me their brand of advice when things have gone wrong? If so, how did I react to that?

_____

_____

_____

_____

_____

_____

_____

_____

> *Miserable comforters are you all! . . . I also could speak like you, if you were in my place. . . . But my mouth would encourage you; comfort from my lips would bring you relief.*
>
> Job 16:2; 4a; 5

Am I teachable in God's eyes? What is the hardest lesson I have learned so far? What did Job learn (see Job 42)?

_____

_____

_____

_____

_____

_____

_____

_____

Teach me to do Your will, for You are my God.

Ps. 143:10a

Week 3

How Can God Help Me Overcome Fear?

SCRIPTURE FOR REFLECTION

The Lord is my light and my salvation—whom shall I fear? The Lord is the stronghold of my life—of whom shall I be afraid? . . . For in the day of trouble He will keep me safe in His dwelling.

Ps. 27:1; 5a

Fear is a favorite weapon of Satan. It goes hand in hand with deception. Our enemy knows that if he can make us afraid and desperate enough, he can get us believing just about anything and keep us from knowing the true peace God wants to give us. What is so devilish about those lies of his is they can contain some half-truths. Then it gets tricky. That's why a well-known acronym for fear is "false evidence appearing real." Satan shows us a great, big, open road, making us fearful and uncertain of the little, curvy, hilly one. But Jesus warned us about the lure of the "broad way" of destruction instead of the "narrow way" of truth. We find that the big superhighway always has a bridge out. It's not what it appears. What we often fail to realize is that God can make the other road into a straight path for us.

Are you sometimes afraid to trust God? Do you find yourself in the "traffic jams" of life because everybody else seems to be traveling that way? That freeway—the broad way—can get pretty clogged up because human nature wants the shortest route. God can help us get off that freeway onto a side road—the narrow way that goes around the trouble. Have you been down any "dead-end roads" lately? God will help us avoid them if we will only put our trust in Him.

QUESTIONS TO THINK ABOUT AND JOURNAL ON THIS WEEK

Can I think of a time when I took a "wrong turn" that looked like the right one? How did I find out my mistake?

_____

_____

_____

_____

_____

_____

_____

> *Satan himself masquerades as an angel of light. It is not surprising, then, if his servants masquerade as servants of righteousness.*
>
> 2 Cor. 11:14–15

What fears do I have? Am I willing to ask God to help me live more courageously?

_____

_____

_____

_____

_____

_____

_____

_____

_____

_____

So we say with confidence, "The Lord is my helper; I will not be afraid. What can man do to me?"

Heb. 13:6

Some fear is healthy and keeps us safe, while other fear is unjustified. In what way has a particular fear protected me?

_____

_____

_____

_____

_____

_____

_____

Be very careful, then, how you live—not as unwise but as wise, making the most of every opportunity, because the days are evil.

Eph. 5:15–16

What are some obstacles in my life that sometimes interfere with my seeing the truth?

_____

_____

_____

_____

_____

_____

_____

_____

Let no one deceive you with empty words, for because of such things, God's wrath comes on those who are disobedient. Therefore, do not be partners with them.

Eph. 5:6–7

Do I understand Satan's power to deceive me? Have I ever been deceived?

_____

_____

_____

_____

_____

_____

_____

And there was war in heaven. . . . The great dragon was hurled down—that ancient serpent called the devil or Satan, who leads the whole world astray.

Rev. 12:7a; 9

Is it easier for me to see fear and deception in somebody else's life than in my own? Why or why not?

_____

_____

_____

_____

_____

_____

_____

Why do you look at the speck of sawdust in your brother's eye and pay no attention to the plank in your own eye?

Matt. 7:3

How does Psalm 27 comfort and reassure me? Which verse or verses do I particularly like?

_____

_____

_____

_____

_____

_____

_____

*I am still confident of this: I will see the good-
ness of the Lord in the land of the living. Wait for
the Lord; be strong and take heart and wait for
the Lord.*

Ps. 27:13–14

READER/CUSTOMER CARE SURVEY

FEFC

We care about your opinions! Please take a moment to fill out our online Reader Survey at **http://survey.hcibooks.com**. As a **"THANK YOU"** you will receive a **VALUABLE INSTANT COUPON** towards future book purchases as well as a **SPECIAL GIFT** available only online! Or, you may mail this card back to us and we will send you a copy of our exciting catalog with your valuable coupon inside.

(PLEASE PRINT IN ALL CAPS)

First Name		MI.	Last Name

Address			City

State	Zip	Email	

1. Gender
- ❑ Female   ❑ Male

2. Age
- ❑ 8 or younger
- ❑ 9-12   ❑ 13-16
- ❑ 17-20   ❑ 21-30
- ❑ 31+

3. Did you receive this book as a gift?
- ❑ Yes   ❑ No

4. Annual Household Income
- ❑ under $25,000
- ❑ $25,000 - $34,999
- ❑ $35,000 - $49,999
- ❑ $50,000 - $74,999
- ❑ over $75,000

5. What are the ages of the children living in your house?
- ❑ 0 - 14   ❑ 15+

6. Marital Status
- ❑ Single
- ❑ Married
- ❑ Divorced
- ❑ Widowed

7. How did you find out about the book?
(please choose one)
- ❑ Recommendation
- ❑ Store Display
- ❑ Online
- ❑ Catalog/Mailing
- ❑ Interview/Review

8. Where do you usually buy books?
(please choose one)
- ❑ Bookstore
- ❑ Online
- ❑ Book Club/Mail Order
- ❑ Price Club (Sam's Club, Costco's, etc.)
- ❑ Retail Store (Target, Wal-Mart, etc.)

9. What subject do you enjoy reading about the most?
(please choose one)
- ❑ Parenting/Family
- ❑ Relationships
- ❑ Recovery/Addictions
- ❑ Health/Nutrition
- ❑ Christianity
- ❑ Spirituality/Inspiration
- ❑ Business Self-help
- ❑ Women's Issues
- ❑ Sports

10. What attracts you most to a book?
(please choose one)
- ❑ Title
- ❑ Cover Design
- ❑ Author
- ❑ Content

TAPE IN MIDDLE; DO NOT STAPLE

NO POSTAGE
NECESSARY
IF MAILED
IN THE
UNITED STATES

BUSINESS REPLY MAIL

FIRST-CLASS MAIL PERMIT NO 45 DEERFIELD BEACH, FL

POSTAGE WILL BE PAID BY ADDRESSEE

Faith Communications, Inc.
3201 SW 15th Street
Deerfield Beach FL 33442-9875

FOLD HERE

Comments

WeeK 4

Why Does God Allow Tough Times?

SCRIPTURE FOR REFLECTION

Therefore, since Christ suffered in his body, arm yourselves also with the same attitude, because he who has suffered in his body is done with sin. As a result, he does not live the rest of his earthly life for evil human desires, but rather for the will of God.

1 Peter 4:1–2

As we have already seen, there is no guarantee of happiness or ease in this life, although we will certainly have our share of happiness. Does God want us to have happiness and to know certain pleasures? Of course. Remember, His original creation was a paradise. Yet our enemy wants to thwart God's plans at every turn. The presence of sin and evil in the world means that we must experience pain and heartache from time to time. There is a promise for victory, however. "In this world, you will have trouble," Jesus tells us. "But take heart! I have overcome the world" (John 16:33). When the darkness threatens to overwhelm us, Jesus asks us to look to him, the "light of the world," for peace and assurance.

Do you ever "bite off more than you can chew" in trying to solve your own problems? We can't expect all our problems to

121

go away. They are part of life. What God wants is for us to stop being Rambo and let Him help us fight our battles. We'll get wounded occasionally, but these "war wounds" will put us in good company. Not only will we identify with other Christians who have suffered, but also with Jesus, himself. Suffering helps us to grow stronger and gives us the ability to comfort others who also suffer.

QUESTIONS TO THINK ABOUT AND JOURNAL ON THIS WEEK

How does suffering help me to "live for the will of God" (1 Peter 4:2)?

_____

_____

_____

_____

_____

_____

_____

Therefore, since Christ suffered in his body, arm yourselves also with the same attitude, because he who has suffered in his body is done with sin. As a result, he does not live the rest of his earthly life for evil human desires, but rather for the will of God.

1 Peter 4:1–2

Is happiness my main goal in life? If so, how do I intend to achieve it?

_____

_____

_____

_____

_____

_____

Where there is no vision, the people are unre-strained, but happy is he who keeps the law.

Prov. 29:18 NASB

Have I ever wanted something very badly and then, after getting it, discovered that it no longer interested me? Why was that?

_____

_____

_____

_____

_____

_____

My heart took delight in all my work, and this was the reward for all my labor. Yet when I sur-veyed all that my hands had done and what I had toiled to achieve, everything was meaning-less, a chasing after the wind.

Eccl. 2:10–11

When did I last overcome a difficult problem or challenge? How did I feel afterward? Did I do it on my own, or did I have some help or encouragement?

_____

_____

_____

_____

_____

_____

I can do everything through him who gives me strength.

Phil. 4:13

What do I see as my strongest personality trait? What is my weakest? How can I strengthen my weaker areas?

_____

_____

_____

_____

_____

My grace is sufficient for you, for my power is made perfect in weakness.

2 Cor. 12:9

Do I sometimes put unusual pressure on myself to achieve or measure up to other's expectations? If so, why do I think that is?

_____

_____

_____

_____

_____

_____

_____

May the words of my mouth and the meditations of my heart be pleasing in your sight, oh Lord, my rock and my redeemer.

Ps. 19:14

Am I an encourager to others, or do I feel instead that everyone should "stand on his own feet"? Why or why not?

_____

_____

_____

_____

_____

_____

Therefore, encourage one another and build each other up, just as in fact you are doing.

1 Thess. 5:11

Month 6

SALVATION: SPIRITUAL REBIRTH THROUGH JESUS

The human race would be cut off from God and lost in sin if not for the redeeming power of Jesus Christ, God's own son, who came to Earth to live among us, suffering and dying in our place to bridge the gap between God and His rebellious children. Everyone has the hope of healing and salvation through Jesus' death and resurrection.

QUESTIONS TO GUIDE THIS MONTH'S DEVOTIONS

- Who is Jesus, really? How is he unique in all of history?
- Why did Jesus have to be crucified?
- What is "repenting of sin," and why is it necessary?
- What is spiritual rebirth, and how can I have it?

Week 1

Who Is Jesus: Son of God, Son of Man . . . Superhero?

SCRIPTURE FOR REFLECTION

The Word became flesh and made his dwelling among us. We have seen his glory, the glory of the One and Only, who came from the Father, full of grace and truth.

John 1:14

We would be hard-pressed to find an individual in the civilized world today who has not heard of Jesus. Getting everyone to agree on just who he is or was, however, would be another matter altogether. Many people accept Jesus as an historical figure—a great moral teacher or rabbi—but reject the belief that he was God's son during the thirty-three years he lived on Earth. To accept that Jesus was born miraculously of a virgin, the literal son of God, is a leap of faith that many people just can't take. If they can't accept that Jesus is the son of God, they surely will have problems believing that he came back to life following his crucifixion and ascended back to heaven to remain at the right hand of God, the Father.

Why are we asked to accept all this as truth? What was the purpose of Jesus' life and death? What does it mean for you, personally? John's gospel answers those questions in a unique way. The verse above is the entire gospel in compressed form. John emphasizes the divine nature of Jesus and details the miracles that portray Jesus as God's son. "The Word" is another name for Jesus, linking him to God as creator and author of all. It is the truth of the Word that John, beloved disciple of Christ, asks us to accept. Who is Jesus to you—personal Savior or really cool teacher? Do you really know him?

QUESTIONS TO THINK ABOUT AND JOURNAL ON THIS WEEK

How do I accept Jesus? Is he a larger-than-life superhero to me—or merely an exceptional man? Or is he God?

_____

_____

_____

_____

_____

_____

If you knew me, you would know my Father also.

John 8:19

Did I grow up being exposed to Bible stories about Jesus from early childhood, or did I come to know about him later? If I have children of my own one day, will I share the story of Jesus with them?

_____

_____

_____

_____

_____

_____

_____

_____

_____

_____

I tell you the truth, unless you change and become like little children, you will never enter the kingdom of heaven.

Matt. 18:3

Is it hard for me to believe that Jesus never sinned? How does knowing that he was still *tempted* (not sinful) in his humanity while on Earth reassure me as I face temptation?

_____

_____

_____

_____

_____

_____

_____

Then Jesus was led by the Spirit into the desert to be tempted by the devil. After fasting forty days and forty nights, he was hungry. The tempter came to him and said, "If you are the Son of

God, tell these stones to become bread." Jesus answered, "It is written: 'Man does not live on bread alone, but on every word that comes from the mouth of God.'"

Matt. 4:1–4

If I could go back in time and meet Jesus, the man, what one question would I like to ask him?

_____

_____

_____

_____

_____

_____

_____

When Jesus had finished saying these things, the crowds were amazed at this teaching, because he taught as one who had authority, and not as their teachers of the law.

Matt. 7:28–29

Why do I think so many people rejected Jesus, even when they witnessed his miracles firsthand?

_____

_____

_____

_____

_____

_____

_____

_____

This is the verdict: Light has come into the world, but men love darkness instead of light because their deeds were evil.

John 3:19

How has knowing Jesus made a difference in my life, or how do I hope it will make a difference?

_____

_____

_____

_____

_____

_____

_____

Peace I leave with you; my peace I give you. I do not give you as the world gives. Do not let your hearts be troubled and do not be afraid.

John 14:27

What is the significance of John the Baptist's statement about Jesus, "Look, the Lamb of God who takes away the sins of the world!" (John 1:29)?

_____

_____

_____

_____

_____

_____

_____

_____

> *God made him who had no sin to be sin for us, so that in him we might become the righteousness of God.*
>
> 2 Cor. 5:21

Week 2

What Is the Real Significance Behind the Cross?

SCRIPTURE FOR REFLECTION

He said to them, "How foolish you are and how slow of heart to believe all that the prophets have spoken! Did not the Christ have to suffer these things and then enter his glory?"

Luke 24:25–26

"Why must you go away?" the disciples asked Jesus when he first told them of his coming death and resurrection. "Why can't we go with you?" These chosen ones were concerned for their beloved teacher and friend. They couldn't imagine going on without him. Yet, Jesus had to leave them. He had no choice. It had all been determined ages beforehand. They (and we) could not become who they were destined to be unless Jesus redeemed all of mankind and sent God's Holy Spirit to dwell inside each individual who believed. The Spirit would connect us for all time to Jesus and would make his power our own. Like a seed that dies into the ground only to be reborn into a beautiful, flourishing plant, Christ died in order to be reborn into those who love him. He is called the vine, while we are the branches who take our nourishment and life from him. It is the beautiful, simple truth of the ages.

When we identify with Christ's death and resurrection, we inherit the same heavenly kingdom that he has. We become adopted sons or daughters of God, "fellow heirs" with Christ, as the apostle Paul so eloquently reminds us in his letter to the Christians in Rome. Do you get it? It may take a little time to really see why Jesus had to "suffer these things." He loved us that much, and he is patient while we learn.

QUESTIONS TO THINK ABOUT
AND JOURNAL ON THIS WEEK

Have I had problems understanding the real meaning of Jesus' crucifixion? In what ways do I better understand now?

_____

_____

_____

_____

_____

_____

_____

_____

I have been crucified with Christ and I no longer live, but Christ lives in me. The life I live in the body, I live by faith in the Son of God, who loved me and gave himself for me.

Gal. 2:20

Does it seem unfair to me that Jesus, who was innocent, had to suffer and die because mankind had rebelled against God? Why do I think God didn't just abandon the human race and stay content with His heavenly creation?

_____

_____

_____

_____

_____

_____

_____

> *For God so loved the world that He gave his one and only Son, that whoever believes in him shall not perish but have eternal life.*
>
> John 3:16

Do I really understand what it means to be a "fellow heir" with Jesus to all of God's glory? Why would God love me that much?

_____

_____

_____

_____

_____

_____

_____

*Because you are sons, God sent the Spirit of His
Son into our hearts, the Spirit who calls out,
"Abba, Father." You are a son; and since you are
a son, God has made you also an heir.*

Gal. 4:6–7

Have I tried to explain the meaning of Jesus' death and resurrection
to someone? If so, how did that person receive it? Is this month's
study helping me to explain it better?

_____

_____

_____

_____

_____

_____

*We accept man's testimony, but God's testimony
is greater because it is the testimony of God,
which He has given about His son. Anyone who
believes in the Son of God has this testimony in
his heart.*

1 John 5:9–10a

Jesus knew all along that he would have to die on the cross, yet on
the eve of his arrest, he prayed to God that "this cup be taken from
me"—that he might be spared that horrible death—ending his
prayer with, "Yet not as I will, but as You will." How does this prayer
reflect both the human and divine nature of Jesus?

_____

_____

_____

_____

_____

_____

_____

_____

He was despised and rejected by men, a man of sorrows and familiar with suffering. . . . The punishment that brought us peace was upon him, and by his wounds we are healed.

Isa. 53:3a; 5b

John's gospel is the only one of the four that does not include the above prayer by Jesus, but instead records the beautiful prayer known as his "high priestly prayer" for his disciples and for all believers, present and future (John 17). How does knowing that Jesus is interceding in heaven for me right now through that prayer make me feel?

_____

_____

_____

_____

_____

_____

_____

_____

My prayer is not for them alone. I pray also for those who will believe in me through their message, that all of them may be one, Father, just as You are in me and I am in You. May they also be in us so that the world may believe that You have sent me.

John 17:20–21

At the close of Luke 24, just before the risen Lord Jesus ascended back to heaven, he explained to his disciples why he had to be sacrificed for all humanity's sins (Luke 24:45–49). He "opened their minds so they could understand the Scriptures." Has Jesus begun to open my mind through the Holy Spirit this way yet? If so, what do I see now that I didn't before?

_____

_____

_____

_____

_____

_____

_____

He told them, "This is what is written: The Christ will suffer and rise from the dead on the third day, and repentance and forgiveness of sins will be preached in his name to all nations, beginning at Jerusalem."

Luke 24:46–47

Week 3

Why Is Repenting More than Saying "I'm Sorry"?

SCRIPTURE FOR REFLECTION

The son said to him, "Father, I have sinned against heaven and against you. I am no longer worthy to be called your son." But the father said to his servants, "Quick! Bring the best robe and put it on him. . . . Let's have a feast and celebrate. For this son of mine is dead and is alive again; he was lost and is found."

Luke 15:21–24

The story of the prodigal (lost) son is one of the most touching of Jesus' parables in the New Testament. Who cannot relate in some way to the stubborn, independent son who was determined to strike out and live his life on his own terms, no matter the consequences? Surely, his father must have longed for him to come to his senses and return home. He could hardly believe his eyes when he saw this wayward son one day making his way back home. This loving father ran to meet his son before he even got all the way home, so great was his joy at seeing him again. Notice what the son said upon seeing his father. He acknowledged his mistake and the grief he had caused his father. He was even ready to give up his rightful place in the family and work as one of the hired hands. His father would not hear of it. He welcomed him back as if he had never left.

Not all earthly fathers could be so forgiving. God is, how-ever. He goes to the ends of the Earth to breathe His love and forgiveness into our hearts and welcomes us with great rejoic-ing when we repent of our sinful ways and come to Him. To repent is to be more than just sorrowful. It is to be willing to change, no matter what the cost, as the prodigal son was. Have you opened your heart to that kind of repentance? God stands waiting to welcome us with open arms. Will you come and join Him at the banquet table He has set for you?

QUESTIONS TO THINK ABOUT AND JOURNAL ON THIS WEEK

Have I been (or am I still) a "prodigal son"? Have I "come home" yet? Why or why not?

_____

_____

_____

_____

_____

_____

_____

Come to me, all you who are weary and bur-dened, and I will give you rest. Take my yoke upon you and learn from me, for I am gentle and humble in heart, and you will find rest for your souls.

Matt. 11:28–29

Perhaps I'm like the other, faithful son in the story of the prodigal son—the one who never strayed or rebelled against his father's authority (read on in the story). Was he justified in feeling jealous over his father's treatment of the other brother? How would I feel?

_____

_____

_____

_____

_____

_____

_____

> *The older brother became angry and refused to go in. . . . "My son," the father said, "you are always with me, and everything I have is yours. But we had to celebrate and be glad because this brother of yours was dead and is alive again; he was lost and is found."*
>
> Luke 15:28; 31

Do I have something right now for which I need to repent or confess to God? If so, am I ready? What should my prayer of repentance be like?

_____

_____

_____

_____

_____

_____

_____

_____

> *For I know my transgressions, and my sin is always before me. . . . Create in me a pure heart, O God, and renew a steadfast spirit within me.*
>
> Ps. 51:3; 10

Is it impossible to see myself through the eyes of a parent? How about through the eyes of my Heavenly Father? When does my need to be independent become rebellion that hurts my parents—or God?

_____

_____

_____

_____

_____

_____

_____

> *Stop listening to instruction, my son, and you will stray from the words of knowledge.*
>
> Prov. 19:27

Do I feel that I've committed some sin that God would never forgive? Does this month's study help me to feel differently about it?

_____

_____

_____

_____

_____

_____

_____

_____

*He does not treat us as our sins deserve or repay
us according to our iniquities. . . . As far as the
east is from the west, so far as He removed our
transgressions from us.*

                                        Ps. 103:10; 12

Do I know the difference between false guilt (which Satan uses to
imprison me) and conviction (which the Holy Spirit uses to change my
heart)? What has God convicted me of recently? Am I changing it?

_____

_____

_____

_____

_____

_____

_____

*Unless I go away, the Counselor will not come to
you. . . . When He comes, He will convict the
world of guilt in regard to sin and righteousness
and judgment.*

                                        John 16:7–8

Luke 15 also contains two shorter parables that illustrate God's joy over those who repent: the parables of the lost sheep and the lost coin. What do they say about God's willingness to forgive me?

_____

_____

_____

_____

_____

_____

_____

In him we have redemption through his blood, the forgiveness of sins, in accordance with the riches of God's grace that He lavished on us with all wisdom and understanding.

Eph. 1:7–8

Week 4

What Does It Mean to Be "Born Again"?

SCRIPTURE FOR REFLECTION

I tell you the truth, no one can enter the kingdom of God unless he is born again. "How can a man be born when he is old?" Nicodemus asked. Jesus answered, "I tell you the truth, no one can enter the kingdom of God unless he is born of water and the Spirit. Flesh gives birth to flesh, but the Spirit gives birth to spirit."

John 3:3–6

We may be a little more savvy these days than Nicodemus was—we know Jesus didn't mean a literal birth when he said we must be born again—yet the act of becoming a new person from the inside out is no less amazing. It goes deeper than just making a decision to repent or change our ways. It means opening ourselves to being wounded along with Christ, to dying in a sense to our old, stubborn selves and identifying with the resurrection to a new life as a son or daughter of God. The sacrament of water baptism so beautifully captures the symbol of rebirth when we are immersed into water and then brought up, cleansed and ready for a new beginning—"born of water." Although we can't see the moment when it happens, the Holy Spirit then comes into our hearts and we are "born of the Spirit." When John the Baptist baptized Jesus, he observed "the Spirit descending as a dove out of heaven, and He remained upon him" (John 1:32). At this moment, John recognized that Jesus was the son of God, as God had foretold him of this incident, saying, "This is the one who baptizes in the Holy Spirit."

Have you had this experience yet? Does the Holy Spirit live in you as your counselor, comforter and "giver of gifts"? If not, are you ready to be born again? All it takes is one sincere prayer to acknowledge Jesus as your Savior, the first step to a new life in him.

QUESTIONS TO THINK ABOUT
AND JOURNAL ON THIS WEEK

Does the idea of being "born again" seem scary to me? How can I become a new person in Christ, yet still be me?

_____

_____

_____

_____

_____

_____

_____

Whoever wants to save his life will lose it, but whoever loses his life for me will find it. What good will it be for a man if he gains the whole world, yet forfeits his soul?

Matt. 16:25–26

Have I been baptized? If so, what does that mean to me? If not, am
I willing to make the decision to be baptized?

_____

_____

_____

_____

_____

_____

_____

> *Don't you know that all of us who were baptized
> into Christ Jesus were baptized into his death? We
> were therefore buried with him through baptism
> into death in order that, just as Christ was raised
> from the dead through the glory of the Father, we
> too may live a new life.*
>
> Rom. 6:3–4

Am I still confused in any way about the Holy Trinity consisting of
God in three parts—the Father, Son and Holy Spirit? In what way
does this month's study make it clearer to me?

_____

_____

_____

_____

_____

_____

The angel answered, "The Holy Spirit will come
upon you, and the power of the Most High will
overshadow you. So the holy one to be born will
be called the Son of God. . . . For nothing is
impossible with God."

Luke 1:35; 37

Both Jesus and John the Baptist make it very clear in John 3 that those who reject Jesus right to the end are rejecting God and will be condemned. Yet many people insist that they can know God without having to know Jesus as Savior—that Christianity is too narrow. Do I still doubt that Jesus is the one true way to God? Why or why not?

_____

_____

_____

_____

_____

_____

_____

_____

I stand with the Father, who sent me. I am one
and who testifies for myself; my other witness is
the Father, who sent me.

John 8:16b; 18

Can I see now how Jesus' death and resurrection were necessary for me to be completely who God wants me to be—that just as Jesus gave up his earthly life, I must give up my desire to be ruled by the world (or the "flesh")? How would I explain this process in my own words?

_____

_____

_____

_____

_____

_____

_____

If anyone loves the world, the love of the Father is not in him. . . . The world and its desires will pass away, but the man who does the will of God lives forever.

1 John 2:15; 17

Have I truly accepted Jesus Christ as my personal Savior? If I'm not sure, can I pray for that to happen now? My prayer only has to be simple, but sincere. My prayer:

_____

_____

_____

_____

_____

_____

_____

No one has seen the Father except the one who is from God; only he has seen the Father. I tell you the truth, he who believes has everlasting life. I am the bread of life.

John 6:46–48

In John 3:30, John the Baptist (not the same John who wrote the gospel) says about Jesus, "He must become greater; I must become less." How does this statement apply to my life as a Christian?

_____

_____

_____

_____

_____

_____

_____

Then Jesus said to his disciples, "If anyone would come after me, he must deny himself and take up his cross and follow me."

Matt. 16:24

Month 7

LOVE: THE IMPORTANCE OF LETTING OTHERS KNOW I'M A CHRISTIAN

Jesus Christ brought a new commandment to the world—that we love one another as he loved us. The Greek word for this kind of love is *agape*. Christian love is modeled after the love of Jesus and should be at the center of all our relationships. We cannot call ourselves Christians and not have *agape* for our fellow human beings.

QUESTIONS TO GUIDE THIS MONTH'S DEVOTIONS

- What is God's standard for love? Why is the "Golden Rule" important?
- Why does God expect me to forgive, even when it seems impossible?
- What does "self-love" mean? Why should I love myself?
- How can I demonstrate Christian love in all that I do and say—all the time?

Week 1

The Golden Rule: Must I Treat Everyone the Same?

SCRIPTURE FOR REFLECTION

If I speak in the tongues of men and of angels, but have not love, I am only a resounding gong or a clanging cymbal.

1 Cor. 13

When asked by a Jewish lawyer what the greatest commandment in the Jewish Law was, Jesus replied, "'Love the Lord your God with all your heart and with all your soul and with all your mind.' . . . And the second is like it: 'Love your neighbor as yourself'" (Matt. 22:37; 39). In other words, treat others as you want to be treated—the Golden Rule. This emphasis on love was the heart of Jesus' message and was echoed by the apostle Paul in the beautiful passage above. If we love one another as we love God and ourselves, all else will fall into place. Our choices, our relationships and everything we do will reflect that we are Christians—which literally means "little Christ." We are to imitate Jesus Christ in all that we do to the best of our abilities, and to draw on his strength when we reach the end of our human limitations.

It's not the treating-others-as-we-want-to-be-treated part that gets us; rather, it's having to endure being mistreated sometimes. It doesn't seem *fair*: Why should we love our

155

neighbor when he or she treats us so badly? Can that kind of forgiving love really change him or her? Maybe, maybe not. But here's the thing: It's not our responsibility to change anyone. That's God's job, and even He can't do it without the desire on the part of the individual needing to be changed. Our example is to be the same everywhere we go, just as Jesus was. Only then can God work through us to make a difference. Do you live according to the Golden Rule? Are you ready to show that kind of love to others?

QUESTIONS TO THINK ABOUT AND JOURNAL ON THIS WEEK

How does love sometimes overcome hate? Have I had the chance to prove this in any situation? If so, how? What does the phrase "burning coals" (in the verse below) mean?

_____

_____

_____

_____

_____

_____

_____

If your enemy is hungry, feed him; if he is thirsty, give him something to drink. In doing this you will heap burning coals on his head.

Prov. 25:21–22

Have I ever treated someone kindly only to have that person turn around and put me down? If so, why do I think that happened?

_____

_____

_____

_____

_____

_____

> *And as for you brothers, never tire of doing what is right.*
>
> 2 Thess. 3:13

Have I been guilty of not appreciating a kind gesture from a friend or family member? When? Have I returned the kindness, or do I still need to do that?

_____

_____

_____

_____

_____

_____

> *It is more blessed to give than to receive.*
>
> Acts 20:35

How has someone spoken a kind word or done something for me that lifted my spirits when I was down? When have I done this for someone else?

_____

_____

_____

_____

_____

_____

_____

A word aptly spoken is like apples of gold in settings of silver.

Prov. 25:11

Look at 1 Corinthians 13:1–3. What do I think Paul is really saying here?

_____

_____

_____

_____

_____

_____

_____

If I have the gift of prophecy and fathom all mysteries and all knowledge, and if I have a faith

that can move mountains, but have not love I am
nothing.

1 Cor. 13:2

What is the difference between showing compassion to an enemy and allowing myself to be abused by someone who is too filled with hate to receive my kindness?

_____

_____

_____

_____

_____

_____

_____

They repay me evil for good and leave my soul
forlorn. Yet when they were ill, I put on sackcloth
and humbled myself with fasting. . . . Vindicate
me in your righteousness, O Lord my God.

Ps. 35:12–13a; 24

Can I "love my neighbor as myself," as Jesus said in Matthew 22:39, without putting myself in the path of his or her possible hatred? Why or why not?

_____

_____

_____

_____

Dear friends, do not be surprised at the painful trial you are suffering. . . . If you are insulted because of the name of Christ, you are blessed, for the Spirit of glory and of God rests on you.

1 Peter 4:12; 14

Week 2

Must I Always Forgive (Even Those Who I Think Don't Deserve It)?

SCRIPTURE FOR REFLECTION

Then Peter came to Jesus and asked, "Lord, how many times shall I forgive my brother when he sins against me? Up to seven times?" Jesus answered, "I tell you, not seven times, but seventy-seven times."

Matt. 18:21–22

Jesus relates the parable of the unmerciful servant in Matthew's gospel. This is the story of a servant who owed a great sum of money to his master, who took pity on him and mercifully forgave the entire debt. The servant, however, soon forgot this gift. Upon seeing a fellow servant who owed him a small sum, he began choking the man and demanding the money on the spot. When the master heard of this incident, he had the ungrateful servant thrown into prison until he paid the entire original debt.

Jesus used this story to illustrate how we are to forgive each other. The master, of course, represents God and His forgiveness of our overwhelming debt of sin. God is slow to anger, while we tend to go off on others at the slightest crossing of our imaginary line, like the unmerciful servant. Jesus says in

161

Matthew 18 we are to forgive up to seventy-seven times—
that's a lot of forgiving. It sounds impossible until we realize
how many times God is willing to forgive us over our life-
times. Can we follow this example in our relationships with
others? Forgiveness is a two-edged sword. If we want to be
forgiven, we must also forgive. It's just another way of inter-
preting the Golden Rule, isn't it?

QUESTIONS TO THINK ABOUT
AND JOURNAL ON THIS WEEK

Who has been the hardest person to forgive in my life? Am I still
trying or hoping to forgive that person—or I have written him or
her off as unforgivable?

_____

_____

_____

_____

_____

_____

_____

*Jesus said, "Father, forgive them, for they do not
know what they are doing."*

Luke 23; 34

Have I ever said to myself, "I'll forgive, but I won't forget"? Does forgetting mean never to remember the offense again, or to refuse to let it dominate my thoughts?

_____

_____

_____

_____

_____

_____

_____

For I will forgive their wickedness and will remember their sins no more.

Jer. 31:34

The late Corrie ten Boom (who was a prisoner in a Nazi concentration camp) said God places a "No Fishing Allowed" sign where He buries our sins once they are forgiven. Why is it harmful to "fish" there?

_____

_____

_____

_____

_____

_____

_____

For if the message spoken by angels was binding, and every violation and disobedience received its just punishment, how shall we escape if we ignore so great a salvation?

Heb. 2:2–3

Am I in need of forgiveness myself right now for some offense I've committed against another person and, of course, God? What do I plan to do about it?

_____

_____

_____

_____

_____

_____

_____

Hide your face from my sins and blot out all my iniquity. . . . Restore to me the joy of your salvation.

Ps. 51:9; 12

Have I felt that I've had trouble forgiving *myself* for something I've done? Was it an honest mistake or a real sin?

_____

_____

_____

_____

_____

_____

_____

_____

Remember not the sins of my youth and my rebellious ways.

Ps. 25:7a

Has someone been merciful to me, even when I didn't deserve it? If so, what happened? What did I learn from the experience?

_____

_____

_____

_____

_____

_____

_____

Blessed are the merciful, for they shall be shown mercy.

Matt. 5:7

Read Matthew 18:34–35. What do I think the jail and torture represent in this story?

_____

_____

_____

_____

_____

_____

_____

_____

This is how my Heavenly Father will treat each of you unless you forgive your brother from your heart.

Matt. 18:35

Week 3

Do I Feel Worthy of God's Love?

SCRIPTURE FOR REFLECTION

Love your neighbor as yourself.

Mark 12:31

We know we are "fearfully and wonderfully" made in the image of God. That makes us pretty special. But how do we properly respect and love ourselves as creations of God without going overboard and becoming too proud or arrogant? Certainly that was Lucifer's sin in heaven before he was cast to Earth as Satan. As wonderful as we are to God, we are not His equals. Yet He expects us to love others as we love ourselves and to treat them as we want to be treated. If we haven't had the proper example of love from our parents or the people most important to us, we most surely will struggle with our own self-worth. God can love us 24/7, but we won't understand it if someone here on Earth "with skin on," as a little girl once said, doesn't show us God's love.

Loving ourselves means honoring and respecting God's most special creation. Even when those words of Jesus were being recorded in the New Testament two thousand years ago, the Greek language had no word to properly describe what Jesus meant. The word they chose for self-love was *humilitas,* but that referred to a humility that was more like looking down on one's self. It gave too many people permission to feel lower than ants. That's not what God intended. Do you know how to love yourself? God can show you. Then you can extend that same love to others.

QUESTIONS TO THINK ABOUT AND JOURNAL ON THIS WEEK

How do I regard myself—as a special creation of God or as unworthy of love? Why do I feel as I do?

_____

_____

_____

_____

_____

_____

_____

> *What is man that you are mindful of him . . . ?*
> *You made him a little lower than the heavenly*
> *beings and crowned him with glory and honor.*
>
> Ps. 8:4a–5

Who in my life has taught me the most about love? What was the most meaningful lesson? Why was it so meaningful to me?

_____

_____

_____

_____

_____

_____

_____

_____

Where you go I will go and where you stay I will stay. . . . May the Lord deal with me, be it ever so severely, if anything but death separates you and me.

Ruth 1:16–17

Why do I think Jesus placed so much emphasis on loving my neighbor as myself?

_____

_____

_____

_____

_____

_____

_____

The entire law is summed up in a single command: "Love your neighbor as yourself."

Gal. 5:14

Is it possible to love and think highly of someone else if I am down on myself? Why or why not?

_____

_____

_____

_____

_____

_____

> *But I am a worm and not a man, scorned by men and despised by the people. . . . Yet you brought me out of the womb; You made me trust in You even at my mother's breast.*
>
> Ps. 22:6; 9

Have I ever noticed that the flaws in others which drive me crazy are the same flaws I may have? What one thing irritates me the most when I'm around certain people? How can I change that?

_____

_____

_____

_____

_____

_____

Love is patient, love is kind. . . . It is not rude, it is not self-seeking, it is not easily angered, it keeps no record of wrongs.

1 Cor. 13:4a–5

Do I really believe God loves me, no matter what, even when I don't love myself? In what ways does He try to tell me?

_____

_____

_____

_____

_____

_____

_____

For I am convinced that neither death nor life, neither angels nor demons, neither the present nor the future, nor any powers, neither height nor depth, nor anything else in all creation, will be able to separate us from the love of God that is in Christ Jesus our Lord.

Rom. 8:39

In Ephesians 5:29 (see next page), why do I think Jesus compares his love of the church to the care of our own bodies?

_____

_____

_____

_____

_____

_____

_____

_____

After all, no one ever hated his own body, but he feeds and cares for it, just as Christ does the church—for we are members of his body.

Eph. 5:29

Week 4

Why Does God Tell Me Not to Love the World?

SCRIPTURE FOR REFLECTION

My dear children, I write this to you so that you will not sin. But if anybody does sin, we have one who speaks to the Father in our defense— Jesus Christ, the Righteous One. . . . Do not love the world or anything in the world. If anyone loves the world, the love of the Father is not in him.

1 John 2:1; 15

We have to distinguish between loving those who live in the world with us and "loving" the world, or becoming too wrapped up in it. How do we keep the two separate? In the process of associating with those we are trying to influence with the love of Jesus Christ, we may become influenced by them instead. John assures us in the verses above that even when we slip, Jesus—our heavenly attorney—is there to plead our case before the Father. John warns us to be careful, however. Jesus could go out into the world and dine at the tables of sinners because he was the Son of God as well as the Son of Man. We're human and subject to temptations of all sorts, unlike Jesus.

Our best shield against the corruptness of the world, in

addition to daily prayer, is the Word of God, which we carry with us in our hearts. With it we can guard against the "flaming arrows" of Satan, who likes to use other people to get to us. Have you had any of those arrows shot at you lately? Did you have your shield ready? God gives us a life in this world for a relatively brief time. If we learn to focus on where we want to spend eternity, the world will not seem like a constant maze to us.

QUESTIONS TO THINK ABOUT
AND JOURNAL ON THIS WEEK

Am I having a greater influence on my world than it is on me, or is it the other way around?

_____

_____

_____

_____

_____

_____

You, dear children, are from God and have overcome them, because the one who is in you is greater than the one who is in the world.

1 John 4:4

How has the enemy used someone or something in the world to try to trip me up recently? Did I fall or stand steady?

_____

_____

_____

_____

_____

_____

Therefore put on the full armor of God, so that when the day of evil comes, you may be able to stand your ground, and after you have done everything, to stand.

Eph. 6:13

Have my friends who are not Christians made life hard for me because I am a Christian? If so, how should I handle things? What can I say to them?

_____

_____

_____

_____

_____

_____

*For I endure scorn for your sake, and shame cov-
ers my face. . . . For zeal for your house con-
sumes me and the insults of those who insult you
fall on me. . . . May your salvation, O Lord, protect me.*

Ps. 69:7; 9; 29

Is there an area of my life where I have been misled or tempted by
the standards of the world, even though I knew that God's standards
were different? How pressured am I by my friends to do what feels
right or to earn their approval?

_____

_____

_____

_____

_____

_____

_____

*Stay away from a foolish man, for you will not
find knowledge on his lips. The wisdom of the
prudent is to give thought to their ways, but the
folly of fools is deception.*

Prov. 14:7–8

If I knew a friend was considering doing something that is sinful and
destructive in God's eyes, would I care enough to try to convince
that friend not to do it? What would I say?

_____

_____

_____

_____

_____

_____

_____

_____

Brothers, if someone is caught in a sin, you who are spiritual should restore him gently. . . . Carry each other's burdens, and in this way, you will fulfill the law of Christ.

Gal. 6:1a–2

Who in my life has taught me the most about honesty? What did I learn?

_____

_____

_____

_____

_____

_____

_____

But the seed on good soil stands for those with a noble and good heart, who hear the word, retain it, and by persevering produce a crop.

Luke 8:15

Read 1 John 2:4. Do I know people who say they are Christians, yet live as if they are not? How does this affect my desire to be a Christian? How can I guard my faith so as not to weaken it?

_____

_____

_____

_____

_____

_____

_____

You hypocrite, first take the plank out of your eye, and then you will see clearly to remove the speck from your brother's eye.

Luke 6:42b

Month 8

RELATIONSHIPS: GETTING ALONG WITH OTHERS

God demands a higher standard in relationships from Christians than others in the world demand. He wants us to place the needs of others above our own. In doing this, we will know the joy of Christian love.

QUESTIONS TO GUIDE
THIS MONTH'S DEVOTIONS

- In what ways does God's plan for family reflect His character?
- Why does God allow suffering and hardship in our families and close relationships? Will He change things if I ask Him to?
- Does God have a say in the friends I choose—does He "oversee" my friendships?
- How is my relationship with God reflected in my relationships with other people?

WeeK 1

My Family:
What Does God Expect of Me?

SCRIPTURE FOR REFLECTION

Children, obey your parents in the Lord, for this is right. . . . Fathers, do not exasperate your children; instead, bring them up in the training and instruction of the Lord.

Eph. 6:1, 4

Do you feel blessed to have a family? Maybe you don't all live together, and maybe you do. A family is designed by God as the one institution upon which all others are to be modeled. As the health of the family goes, so goes the health of the world. If we think about it, this makes sense. We learn how to relate to others first in our own homes. We learn (hopefully) how to respect authority, how to value the needs of others and how to work as a team. However, even God knows that He can't make families perfect. Because we have the free will to choose how we will live and love, we can make mistakes and hurt each other. When the heads of the household don't act responsibly or according to God's laws, we are then out of kilter, and there is no security. What is your family like? How do you see your place in the household? Do you fit? Are you secure? Do you do all you can to help each family member love and honor each other?

QUESTIONS TO THINK ABOUT
AND JOURNAL ON THIS WEEK

On a scale of 1–10 (with 10 meaning the most harmonious), how do I rate my family? Do we love and respect each other, or are we often thoughtless and careless with each other?

_____

_____

_____

_____

_____

_____

_____

How good and pleasant it is when brothers live together in unity!

Ps. 133:1

Am I responsible for helping to look after a brother or sister? Do I resent it or accept my responsibility without grumbling? Do I willingly do my part to make my family function and be as happy and healthy as it can be? Do I believe I play a part in that, or do I feel it's totally the responsibility of my mom or dad?

_____

_____

_____

_____

_____

_____

_____

> *Then the Lord said to Cain, "Where is your brother Abel?" "I don't know," he replied. "Am I my brother's keeper?"*
>
> Gen. 4:9

What do I know about my family history? Who am I in relation to each of the members in my family?

_____

_____

_____

_____

_____

_____

_____

> *But now the Lord declares: ". . . Those who honor me I will honor, but those who despise me will be disdained."*
>
> 1 Sam. 2:30b

What kinds of rules exist in my family? Am I allowed to set my own limits or are there consequences if I break the rules? How do I feel about this?

_____

_____

_____

_____

_____

_____

_____

_____

We have all had human fathers who disciplined us, and we respected them for it.

Heb. 12:9

If I am troubled or have a problem, do I talk it over with a parent or someone in my family or keep it to myself? Do my parents take time to really listen to me?

_____

_____

_____

_____

_____

_____

_____

Encourage one another and build each other up.

1 Thess. 5:11

Does my family attend church together or have family devotions? If so, do I enjoy these times? Why or why not?

_____

_____

_____

_____

_____

_____

_____

*Listen to my instruction and be wise; do not
ignore it.*

Prov. 8:33

Look at Ephesians 6:1, 4 again. Which do I think happens more
often—a parent exasperating a child or the child disobeying the parent? How does it go in my family? What am I willing to do to not
"provoke" the members of my family?

_____

_____

_____

_____

_____

_____

_____

*Train a child in the way he should go, and when
he is old he will not turn from it.*

Prov. 22:6

Week 2

How Can God Help Me with a Family Crisis?

SCRIPTURE FOR REFLECTION

Who is this who darkens my counsel with words without knowledge? Where were you when I laid the Earth's foundation? Tell me if you understand.

Job 38:2, 4

There isn't a family on Earth that doesn't experience some kind of crisis or upheaval at one time or another. A crisis may come in the form of an unexpected illness, injury or death, a financial setback, a parent choosing to walk out on the family or any poor choice by one member that puts stress and hardship on other members of the family. Chances are, you've experienced one or more of these situations. These tough times never make sense, do they? God doesn't tell us why we must go through hardships, but we know they can strengthen our faith. A great pastor once said, "When you can't trace the hand of God, you can always trust His heart."

A crisis does one of two things to a family—draws it closer together or pulls it apart. These are the times when we find out what we're made of and what real, unconditional love is all about. If we stand shoulder to shoulder, heart to heart against the storm, we can weather it, knowing "this too shall pass." The beauty of family is in making difficulties more bearable as we each carry some of the burden. When we let God comfort us, we then can comfort each other. Each of us brings a particular kind of strength to our family. That is exactly what God had in mind when he designed the family. He modeled this kind of love for us through His son, Jesus. Are you stronger today because of overcoming some crisis in your family? Are you prepared to face the storm that may still be waiting?

QUESTIONS TO THINK ABOUT AND JOURNAL ON THIS WEEK

How has a crisis affected my family? Did we pull together or start to fall apart?

_____

_____

_____

_____

_____

_____

_____

Carry each other's burdens, and in this way you will fulfill the law of Christ.

Gal. 6:2

Do I feel that I play a particular role in my family? Am I the peace-maker, comedian or achiever? How does "playing the part" of one of these roles affect me?

_____

_____

_____

_____

_____

_____

_____

> *There are different kinds of gifts, but the same Spirit. There are different kinds of service, but the same Lord.*
>
> 1 Cor. 12:4

Is it clear whether or not my home follows Jesus' example in loving and supporting each other? How has he made (or how would he make) a difference in my family?

_____

_____

_____

_____

_____

_____

Blessed are the peacemakers, for they will be called sons of God.

Matt. 5:9

If a family member made a choice that caused the rest of the family pain, have I been able to forgive that person? Why or why not?

_____

_____

_____

_____

_____

_____

Be kind and compassionate to one another, forgiving each other, just as Christ God forgave you.

Eph. 5:32

Have I been responsible for bringing a crisis to my family? If so, how did each member react? What did I learn from it?

_____

_____

_____

_____

_____

_____

_____

Godly sorrow brings repentance that leads to salvation and leaves no regret.

2 Cor. 7:10

Do I pray for my family on a regular basis? Do I pray for them at all? How can prayer help us to avoid a future crisis?

_____

_____

_____

_____

_____

_____

_____

Do not be anxious about anything, but in every-thing, by prayer and petition, with thanksgiving, present your requests to God. And the peace of God, which transcends all understanding, will guard your minds and hearts in Christ Jesus.

Phil. 4:6–7

In the book of Job, God allows Satan to test Job's faith through a series of horrible tragedies. Does this seem fair? Job's wife didn't think so. She wanted him to curse God. Job's friends thought they had all the answers. Why do I suppose God allowed Job's temporary afflictions? How do I feel about that?

_____

_____

_____

_____

_____

_____

_____

_____

He replied, "You are talking like a foolish woman. Shall we accept good from God and not trouble?" In all this, Job did not sin in what he said.

Job 2:10

Week 3

Friendships: Am I to Accept Others Just as They Are?

SCRIPTURE FOR REFLECTION

Be completely humble and gentle; be patient, bearing with one another in love. Make every effort to keep the unity of the Spirit through the bond of peace.

Eph. 4:2–3

After family, the most important relationships in our lives are those we have with our friends. In our teen years, friends take on an added significance. It seems at times as if they are the only ones who can understand us. Makes sense. We are usually going through the same struggles and, for the most part, dealing with the same life issues. Because we value their opinions and their support so highly, our friends can make or break us. Can we really be ourselves around our friends, or must we be the people we think they want us to be? Add developing relationships with the opposite sex to this equation, and it gets really confusing. Have you ever lost one or more friends because they were jealous of a new relationship? It happens. They should be happy for you, but instead they worry about never spending time with you again. Who can figure out friends?

The teen years are a time when we form some close bonds, some of which may even last for life. We learn the give and take, the joy and frustration of friendship. We may have to deal with betrayal or shallow values that make certain friends risky business. Likewise, we may know the blessing of encouragement and friends who are literally the "wind beneath our wings." What kinds of friends do you have? Are you better in each other's company? Do you consider God your friend?

QUESTIONS TO THINK ABOUT
AND JOURNAL ON THIS WEEK

Do I have a best or really special friend? What makes me value this person? Do I thank God for blessing my life with this friendship?

_____

_____

_____

_____

_____

_____

_____

There is a friend who sticks closer than a brother.

Prov. 18:24

Is there a time when a friend hurt me or let me down? If so, how did I handle my hurt or anger? Did I talk with God about it?

_____

_____

_____

_____

_____

_____

_____

_____

Do not be overcome by evil, but overcome evil with good.

Rom. 12:21

Do I feel as if I fit in with my peers in school, in church or places where I hang out? Why or why not?

_____

_____

_____

_____

_____

_____

_____

God makes a home for the lonely.

Ps. 68:6a NASB

When a friend whom I respect does something wrong, must I confront that person or would I be afraid of offending him or her or losing the friendship? What would God want me to do should I find myself in such a situation?

_____

_____

_____

_____

_____

_____

_____

_____

*Brothers, if someone is caught in a sin, you who
are spiritual should restore him gently.*

Gal. 6:1

How would I feel if a good friend pointed out that I needed to make
a certain change in an area of my life? Would I feel that person
didn't accept me as I am or would I feel helped and supported?

_____

_____

_____

_____

_____

_____

Wounds from a friend can be trusted.

Prov. 27:6

Am I willing to share my faith with a friend? Do I need someone to talk to me about God instead?

_____

_____

_____

_____

_____

_____

_____

I am not ashamed of the gospel because it is the power of God for the salvation of everyone who believes.

Rom. 1:16

Ephesians 4–5 speaks of the responsibilities of Christian fellowship that come with laying aside the "old self" and growing up our "new self" in Christ. Am I allowed to go by the world's rules when dealing with people outside the church who don't respect Christ's rules? Why or why not?

_____

_____

_____

_____

_____

_____

_____

Live as children of light . . . and find out what pleases the Lord. Have nothing to do with the fruitless deeds of darkness, but rather expose them.

Eph. 5:8b, 10–11

Week 4

Special Someones: Is God Watching?

SCRIPTURE FOR REFLECTION

Father, I want those You have given me to be with me where I am, and to see my glory, the glory You have given me because You loved me before the creation of the world.

John 17:24

By now, most of us have seen WWJD (What Would Jesus Do?). Is it just a trite marketing phrase or a valid question? The New Testament gives us enough insight into the life of Jesus that we can apply his example to almost any situation, including relationships—even special ones. In the gospel of John, Jesus demonstrates *compassion* (preventing the prostitute from being stoned), *protection and self-sacrifice* (the watchful shepherd guarding his sheep), *prayerful intercession* (praying for God's will for his disciples and all future generations of believers) and *forgiveness and restoration* (countering Peter's denial of him and asking him to "feed my sheep"). All these are qualities of unconditional love, which is the heart of any worthwhile relationship. If we think we can make our own rules, we'll be disappointed. How would Jesus handle the relationship challenges in your life? Can you use his example of

Christian love as the measuring stick for *all* your relationships? How are you doing?

QUESTIONS TO THINK ABOUT
AND JOURNAL ON THIS WEEK

What is the biggest challenge I am facing in a relationship? Is it
with a parent or family member? A friend? A teacher or someone I
respect as a mentor? Someone I "have feelings for"?

_____

_____

_____

_____

_____

_____

> *Love is patient, love is kind. It does not envy, it
> does not boast, it is not proud. It is not rude, it is
> not self-seeking, it is not easily angered, it keeps
> no record of wrongs.*
>
> 1 Cor. 13:4–5

How could Jesus' example help me to improve my relationships? Am
I willing to give his way a try?

_____

_____

_____

_____

_____

_____

_____

_____

A new commandment I give you: Love one another. As I have loved you, so you must love one another.

John 13:34

If I felt any friendship was unhealthy for me, would I be willing to drop it? Has this ever happened to me? If so, why? Would I be willing to ask my friend, "Can we pray on it?"—to ask God to help make it clear what we should do?

_____

_____

_____

_____

_____

_____

Do not be yoked together with unbelievers. For what do righteousness and wickedness have in common? Or what fellowship can light have with darkness?

2 Cor. 6:14

Have I shown compassion to someone who is normally rejected by others? Who needs that kind of help from me? Am I willing to do something about it? Have I prayed for this person?

_____

_____

_____

_____

_____

_____

Live in harmony with one another. Do not be proud, but be willing to associate with people of low position. Do not be conceited.

Rom. 12:16

Have I taken the time to pray for and encourage a friend who is hurting? Here is my prayer:

_____

_____

_____

_____

_____

_____

Oil and perfume make the heart glad; so a man's counsel is sweet to his friend.

Prov. 27:9 NASB

Have I forgiven a person in my life who wronged me? Have we restored that relationship? Why or why not?

_____

_____

_____

_____

_____

_____

_____

If anyone says, "I love God," yet hates his brother, he is a liar. For anyone who does not love his brother, whom he has seen, cannot love God, whom he has not seen.

1 John 4:20

Look at John 21:15–19. Do I believe Peter was more hurt or ashamed by Jesus' questioning of him, considering he had denied knowing Jesus prior to his crucifixion? Remember, this is the resurrected Christ speaking with Peter. Did Peter accept Jesus' forgiveness? What is the lesson in this that can be applied to my life?

_____

_____

_____

_____

_____

_____

_____

_____

The third time he said to him, "Simon, son of John, do you love me?" He answered, "Yes, Lord, you know that I love you." Peter was hurt because Jesus asked him the third time, "Do you love me?"

John 21:17

Month 9

GRACE: GOD'S AMAZING GIFT TO ME

God grants each of His children the gift of His grace as a way of demonstrating His love for us. His grace is given to us to help us through life's trials and even to show us how to properly handle its successes. It is available for us every day, no matter how much we already have received. As long as we have faith in Christ, we can never run out of God's grace.

QUESTIONS TO GUIDE
THIS MONTH'S DEVOTIONS

- What is grace, and how does God make His grace available to me?
- Does God really provide an escape route from temptation for me?
- What is the "fruit of the Spirit," and how do I know if these character traits are mine?
- Can I do something so bad that God will turn away from me?

WeeK 1

What Is Grace, and How Do I Get It?

SCRIPTURE FOR REFLECTION

For if the many died by the trespass of the one man, how much more did God's grace and the gift that came by the grace of the one man, Jesus Christ, overflow to the many! . . . But where sin increased, grace increased all the more, so that just as sin reigned in death, so also grace might reign through righteousness to bring eternal life through Jesus Christ our Lord.

Rom. 5:15; 20–21

The book of Romans, a letter written to the early Christians in Rome from the apostle Paul, is probably the most powerful testimony to God's grace in all of the New Testament. Paul was trained in the law, so he was highly skilled at using logic to lay out his argument for God, much as an attorney would argue his case before a court. Today, we might call him an "apologist." His modern equivalent probably would be someone like the late C. S. Lewis who, like Paul, was educated, intelligent and had a dramatic conversion in adulthood to Christianity.

Grace comes to us through God's Holy Spirit, the "giver of gifts," who keeps us closely connected to God. Have you suffered a loss or tragedy of some kind? Grace can give you the ability to come to terms with it and know God's peace. Have you been unusually blessed in some way? This also is a gift of grace. When Paul wrote, "I can do everything through Him who gives me strength" (Phil. 4:13), he was referring to God's all-sufficient grace, no matter what the circumstances of his life. If we know God, we are automatically assured of His grace in all situations, no matter how weak or strong we feel. He knows just how much we need and when we need it. His grace never fails. Amazing, isn't it? God loves us so much!

QUESTIONS TO THINK ABOUT
AND JOURNAL ON THIS WEEK

When did God's grace get me through a tough situation? What happened? Did I thank God for helping me out?

_____

_____

_____

_____

_____

_____

_____

Come near to God and He will come near to you. . . . Humble yourselves before the Lord, and he will lift you up.

James 4:8; 10

Do I have trouble believing that I don't have to do anything to deserve God's grace? Why or why not?

_____

_____

_____

_____

_____

_____

_____

_____

> *He who did not spare His own Son, but gave him up for us all—how will He not also, along with him, graciously give us all things?*
>
> Rom. 8:32

The apostle Paul wrote in the New Testament of an unspecified "thorn in the flesh" that God had given him to keep him humble and close to Him. God did not take it away, even after Paul prayed for it several times. Instead, God gave Paul the verse below. What is my thorn, if I have one?

_____

_____

_____

_____

_____

_____

_____

My grace is sufficient for you, for my power is made perfect in weakness.

2 Cor. 12:9

Do I try to handle problems on my own instead of asking for God's help? If so, how does knowing more about God's grace change my thinking?

_____

_____

_____

_____

_____

_____

_____

God opposes the proud, but gives grace to the humble.

Prov. 3:34

In what ways does God's grace help me in dealing with other people?

_____

_____

_____

_____

_____

_____

_____

_____

*Do nothing out of selfish ambition or vain con-
ceit, but in humility consider others better than
yourselves.*

Phil. 2:3

Godly humility, as expressed in Philippians 2:3, is not an easy thing
to live. It doesn't mean I'm a doormat, but rather that I put the needs
of others above my own and refuse to be self-important. What do I
need to change in my relationships, now that I know this?

_____

_____

_____

_____

_____

_____

_____

*When pride comes, then comes disgrace, but
with humility comes wisdom.*

Prov. 11:2

Paul says in Romans 5:1–2 that we gain access to God's grace
through our faith in Christ; we can *do* nothing to deserve it on our

own. If I took the "pulse" of my faith right now, how would it register—strong and steady or weak and failing? Why?

_____

_____

_____

_____

_____

_____

_____

Therefore, since we have been justified through faith, we have peace with God through our Lord Jesus Christ, through whom we have gained access by faith into this grace in which we now stand.

Rom. 5:2

Week 2

How Can I Overcome Temptation?

SCRIPTURE FOR REFLECTION

No temptation has seized you except what is common to man; and God is faithful; He will not let you be tempted beyond what you can bear. But when you are tempted, He will also provide a way out so that you can stand up under it.

1 Cor. 10:13

Notice the last four words in the verse above. God is not necessarily going to just remove temptation from us, or even remove us from it. What He will do, however, is give us the strength to withstand it—to *stand up under it* and resist it. In other words, He gives us the grace to avoid giving in to temptation. Remember, we are always to be covered by the "armor of God" so that we are ready to stand firm against temptation. God may bring to mind a verse of Scripture to encourage us or the ability to see the unpleasant consequences for what we're considering. Whatever He uses, it will be just what we need. The choice to resist will then be ours. When we're tempted, we can let it control us, or we can do as the Bible tells us to do: Take it to God through prayer. Are you willing to do that?

QUESTIONS TO THINK ABOUT
AND JOURNAL ON THIS WEEK

How have I been tempted recently, either in my thoughts or my actions? What did I do about it?

_____

_____

_____

_____

_____

_____

Each one is tempted when, by his own evil desire, he is dragged away and enticed. Then after desire has conceived, it gives birth to sin.

James 1:14–15a

Do I believe that it's easier or harder for a Christian to be tempted? Why? Do I believe God sometimes allows temptation to test my faith?

_____

_____

_____

_____

_____

_____

_____

Simon, Simon, Satan has asked to sift you as wheat. But I have prayed for you, Simon, that your faith may not fail. And when you have turned back, strengthen your brothers.

Luke 22:32–32

What is the one area of my life in which I face the most temptation: pride, laziness, sex, drugs or alcohol, pornography—or something else? Have I asked God to help me overcome it?

_____

_____

_____

_____

_____

_____

_____

Remember not the sins of my youth and my rebellious ways; according to your love, remember me, for you are good, O Lord.

Ps. 25:7

Has there been a time when God through His grace really did help me to escape from a temptation? If so, how did He do it?

_____

_____

_____

_____

_____

_____

_____

_____

I will instruct you and teach you in the way you should go; I will counsel you and watch over you.

Ps. 32:8

Do I have friends who are struggling with various temptations in their lives? How would God want me to help—or not?

_____

_____

_____

_____

_____

_____

_____

Whoever loves his brother lives in the light, and there is nothing in him to make him stumble.

1 John 2:10

Am I most open to temptations after I've had some kind of victory or growth in my spiritual life? Why do I think this happens?

_____

_____

_____

_____

_____

_____

_____

_____

> *Pride goes before destruction, a haughty spirit before a fall.*
>
> Prov. 16:18

In 1 Corinthians 10, Paul writes about the sinful history of the Jewish people as an example for the early Christians in Corinth. How is God using the life of someone I know as an example of what I should not do?

_____

_____

_____

_____

_____

_____

_____

Now these things occurred as examples to keep us from setting our hearts on evil things as they did.

1 Cor. 10:6

Week 3

What Is the "Fruit of the Spirit"?

SCRIPTURE FOR REFLECTION

So I say, live by the Spirit and you will not grat-ify the desires of the sinful nature. For the sinful nature desires what is contrary to the Spirit. . . . But the fruit of the Spirit is love, joy, peace, patience, kindness, goodness, faithfulness, gentleness and self-control. Against such things there is no law.

Gal. 5:16–17a; 22–23

The most overwhelming gift of grace God has offered to believers is the gift of the indwelling Holy Spirit as our helper, comforter, counselor, teacher and giver of spiritual gifts. Paul gave us a list of the qualities that Christians should possess as evidence that the Holy Spirit is living in them, as we see in the verse above. These are known as the "fruit of the Spirit." They are the standard we reach for as we seek to be more like Jesus Christ. In fact, they are qualities of God's own character. Does anyone really display all these qualities all the time? No way! We slip up because we're human. If we were perfect and able to be all those things Paul describes all the time, why would we even need God's grace? Still, that doesn't mean God doesn't want us to do our best to reflect the fruit of the Spirit in all that we do. Paul told the early Christians to test their faith by examining themselves to see if Christ really was in them. Do you do this for yourself? Do you keep tabs on your spiritual life or do you ignore it? Do you leave "spiritual life" for church on Sunday? Are you ready to put the care of your spiritual life as the first priority in your life?

QUESTIONS TO THINK ABOUT
AND JOURNAL ON THIS WEEK

Which fruit of the Spirit shows in my life? In what way?

_____

_____

_____

_____

_____

_____

_____

We have not received the spirit of the world but the Spirit who is from God, that we may understand what God has freely given us.

1 Cor. 2:12

Do I feel it's silly or pointless to even attempt to live by the fruit of the Spirit—that it's just too hard? Why or why not?

_____

_____

_____

_____

_____

_____

_____

The man without the Spirit does not accept the things that come from the Spirit of God, for they are foolishness to him, and he cannot understand them because they are spiritually discerned.

1 Cor. 2:14

Who do I know as the best example of the fruit of the Spirit? Do I put that person on a pedestal as someone I could never be like, or do I strive to be like that person?

_____

_____

_____

_____

_____

_____

*I have set you an example that you should do as
I have done for you. . . . Now that you know
these things, you will be blessed if you do them.*

John 13:15; 17

Do I feel I am responsible for having a positive influence on others
through my life? Who may be watching me and wondering if the
Christian life is for him or her?

_____

_____

_____

_____

_____

_____

*Don't let anyone look down on you because you
are young, but set an example for the believers
in speech, in life, in love, in faith and in purity.*

1 Tim. 4:12

Do I believe that the Holy Spirit actually protects me from sinful
desires? Has he ever done that for me? If so, how?

_____

_____

_____

_____

_____

_____

_____

_____

My prayer is not that You take them out of the world, but that You protect them from the evil one.

John 17:15

What is the one fruit of the Spirit that really contains all the others? Why?

_____

_____

_____

_____

_____

_____

_____

_____

And now these three remain: faith, hope and love. But the greatest of these is love.

1 Cor. 13:13

Look at Galations 5:22 again. Why do I think Paul added "against such things there is no law"? What kind of law was he referring to?

_____

_____

_____

_____

_____

_____

_____

_____

But if you are led by the Spirit, you are not under the law.

Gal. 5:18

Week 4

Does God Ever Get Exasperated with Me?

SCRIPTURE FOR REFLECTION

The Lord is with me; I will not be afraid. What can man do to me? The Lord is with me; He is my helper. I will look in triumph on my enemies.

Ps. 118:6–7

Do you ever doubt that God is really with you? He can seem so far away when we are hurting. Deep down inside, a part of us believes we really don't deserve that kind of God, and we don't. We can't do anything to earn God's love. He just loves us unconditionally. Period. He's the perfect, ultimate Father. People in our lives can and will abandon us, but God never will.

What happens when we try to walk out on God? There's no place where we can hide from Him. We're never out of His sight, but we can put Him out of ours. The more we stray from God, the harder it is to find Him, but it is never impossible. We may think He has forgotten us or that He is punishing us in some way. Oh, He may test us and discipline us to make us stronger—what loving parent wouldn't? He won't protect us from the consequences of our actions, however. Why should He? How else could we learn? We must remember that love is a two-way street. God wants our love, too. He wants us to come to Him and give Him the chance to show us how much He loves us. Are you willing to do that, even when you feel unlovable? Jesus will never stop praying that powerful prayer in John 17 for us. That's the beauty of God's grace. Pretty awesome, isn't it?

QUESTIONS TO THINK ABOUT AND JOURNAL ON THIS WEEK

Have I ever given up on God? Why? What happened?

_____

_____

_____

_____

_____

_____

_____

He is patient with you, not wanting anyone to perish but everyone to come to repentance.
2 Peter 3:9

In what way does learning more about the Word of God help me to want to have a better relationship with God?

_____

_____

_____

_____

_____

_____

_____

_____

I lift up my eyes to the hills—where does my help come from? My help comes from the Lord, the Maker of heaven and Earth.

Ps. 121:1–2

Have I ever felt as if I've committed an unpardonable sin—something that God couldn't possibly forgive? If so, why would I feel that way?

_____

_____

_____

_____

_____

_____

_____

_____

But You, O Lord, are a compassionate and gracious God, slow to anger, abounding in love and faithfulness.

Ps. 86:15

Have I prayed a prayer that I feel God hasn't answered? Am I sure?
If so, what does God's silence mean to me?

_____

_____

_____

_____

_____

_____

_____

> *My soul thirsts for God, for the living God. When can I go and meet with God? My tears have been my food day and night, while men say to me all day long, "Where is your God?"*
>
> Ps. 42:2–3

Do I believe that God puts roadblocks in my path to bring me back
if I'm wandering? Has He done this for me? If so, how?

_____

_____

_____

_____

_____

_____

_____

I will praise the Lord who counsels me; even at night my heart instructs me. . . . You have made known to me the path of life.

Ps. 16:7; 11a

How does my perception of my earthly father affect my relationship with God? Does it make it easier or harder?

_____

_____

_____

_____

_____

_____

_____

For you did not receive a spirit that makes you a slave again to fear, but you received the Spirit of sonship. And by Him, we cry Abba [Daddy], Father. The Spirit Himself testifies that we are God's children.

Rom. 8:15–16

Do I feel as if my "enemies" sometimes get the better of me? How does Psalm 118 reassure me about this?

_____

_____

_____

_____

_____

_____

_____

_____

*I was pushed back and about to fall, but the Lord
helped me. The Lord is my strength and my song;
He has become my salvation.*

Ps. 118:13–14

Month 10

STEWARDSHIP: GIVING BACK TO GOD WHAT IS HIS

Everything we have really belongs to God. We are simply His managers or stewards of it. God blesses us to increase our ability to give back to Him and His kingdom. Our true treasure is in heaven.

We are to live our lives on Earth not to gain temporary material wealth, but to gain a lasting reward in heaven.

QUESTIONS TO GUIDE THIS MONTH'S DEVOTIONS

- How does God expect me to manage what He has given me?
- What is tithing, and how am I to do it?
- Am I to be a "good steward" of my time as well as of my money?
- How does God expect me to witness—and if so, what am I to do?

Week 1

What Do I Know About the "First Bank of Heaven"?

SCRIPTURE FOR REFLECTION

Peter answered him, "We have left everything to follow you! What then will there be for us?" Jesus said to them, "I tell you the truth, at the renewal of all things when the Son of Man sits on his glorious throne, you who have followed me will also sit on twelve thrones, judging the twelve tribes of Israel. And everyone who has left houses or brothers or sisters or father or mother or children or fields for my sake will receive a hundred times as much and will inherit eternal life."

Matt. 19:27–29

Jesus' disciples left behind their former lives and all they owned to follow and serve him. Could we do that if Jesus appeared before us today? He is not really going to ask us to give up everything for him, but he does want us to release our tight grips on anything that prevents us from loving him and doing his will. In other words, he expects us to be willing to give it up if he should ask us to do so. If God should see fit to take or withhold anything from us, it is only because He has something so much better in store for us. He doesn't want us to miss it because we are focused on the here and now and the temporary things of this life.

An old farmer once said, "I never saw a hearse pulling a U-Haul trailer." No, we don't get to take anything with us when we die. We came into the world without belongings, and that's how we're going out. But what is waiting for us is glorious beyond anything we can imagine. What we give up here actually goes into a heavenly bank account that is multiplied a hundred times in the next life! And that life goes on forever! What a concept. We are to give with no thought of a reward here on Earth—even though God may generously bless us in this life—but we can surely expect our reward in heaven if we love God. Jesus guarantees it. How is your attitude toward giving and serving? Do you need to make any changes?

QUESTIONS TO THINK ABOUT
AND JOURNAL ON THIS WEEK

Do I find that I am really focused on the "now" of my life? Am I building my bank account on Earth instead of in heaven? If so, in what ways?

_____

_____

_____

_____

_____

_____

_____

Watch out! Be on your guard against all kinds of greed; a man's life does not consist in the abundance of his possessions.

Luke 12:15

Suppose I felt Jesus was asking me to give up something really important to me, like an opportunity for recognition or something I own? Could I do it? Why or why not?

_____

_____

_____

_____

_____

_____

_____

If anyone would come after me, he must deny himself and take up his cross daily and follow me. For whoever wants to save his life will lose it, but whoever loses his life for me will save it.

Luke 9:23–24

How do I feel when I see someone whose total focus in life is on gaining wealth and then doesn't use it to glorify God? What is the lesson I can use in my own life?

_____

_____

_____

_____

_____

_____

_____

What good is it for a man to gain the whole
world and yet lose or forfeit his very self?

Luke 9:25

We are told to "love people and use things" instead of the other way
around. Have I ever made the mistake of getting that backwards?
How? When I fall short, do I ask God to help me get my priorities
right?

_____

_____

_____

_____

_____

_____

_____

For the love of money is a root of all kinds of
evil. Some people, eager for money, have
wandered from the faith and pierced themselves
with many griefs.

1 Tim. 6:10

What is the most important or valuable thing in my life? Is it a possession, a goal, a person? Am I more committed to it than I am to God? What can I do if my priorities are out of balance?

_____

_____

_____

_____

_____

_____

_____

Godliness with contentment is great gain. For we brought nothing into this world and we take nothing out of it.

1 Tim. 6:6–7

In what ways does the world encourage me to focus on materialism and living for today? Do I ask God to help me align my will with His?

_____

_____

_____

_____

_____

_____

They promise them freedom, while they them-
selves are slaves of depravity—for a man is a
slave to whatever has mastered him.

2 Peter 2:19

Why did Jesus say in Matthew 19:24 that it is "easier for a camel to go through the eye of a needle than for a rich man to enter heaven"? In what ways does this apply to my life?

_____

_____

_____

_____

_____

_____

_____

I tell you the truth, it is hard for a rich man to
enter the kingdom of heaven.

Matt. 19:23

Week 2

Tithing: What Exactly Is Expected of Me?

SCRIPTURE FOR REFLECTION

"Bring the whole tithe into the storehouse, that there may be food in my house. Test me in this," says the Lord Almighty, *"and see if I will not throw open the floodgates of heaven and pour out so much blessing that you will not have room enough for it."*

Mal. 3:10

Tithing, or the giving back to God through His church one-tenth of our income or material blessings, goes hand in hand with the principle of stewardship. Many people give offerings from time to time, or place some money in the collection plate when it is passed, but do we consistently give one-tenth of our earnings? God expects us to. He rebuked the Jewish nation at the close of the Old Testament for refusing to give "the whole tithe." In fact, He said they were *robbing* Him. He promised them through the prophet Malachi that He would pour great material blessings upon them if they would obey His command to tithe, but that they would live under a curse if they held back. God must take tithing pretty seriously, then.

How can we get on track with our giving? Why would God even care since we don't have much to give anyway? He's not interested in how much we can give; He just wants us to offer His portion back with a thankful heart, realizing that it all comes from Him anyway. If a neighbor did something really kind and generous for us while we were sick, we naturally would want to do something nice in return, wouldn't we? Can we have that same attitude toward God? By tithing, we honor God's generosity and make ourselves available for even bigger blessings. God tells us to test Him in this. What is your plan for doing that?

QUESTIONS TO THINK ABOUT AND JOURNAL ON THIS WEEK

Do I believe that God only expects those who are well-off to tithe? Why or why not?

_____

_____

_____

_____

_____

_____

_____

Rich and poor have this in common: The Lord is the Maker of them all.

Prov. 22:2

If I already have tested God's promise about tithing, what kind of blessing did I receive?

_____

_____

_____

_____

_____

_____

_____

> *Give, and it will be given to you. A good measure, pressed down, shaken together and running over, will be poured into your lap.*
>
> Luke 6:38

Why do I think tithing is so important to God?

_____

_____

_____

_____

_____

_____

_____

> *Do not be deceived: God cannot be mocked. A man reaps what he sows.*
>
> Gal. 6:7

Why is it so hard for most people to tithe? Do we get a false sense of security by keeping everything for ourselves? Is this true for me?

_____

_____

_____

_____

_____

_____

> *Whoever loves money never has money enough; whoever loves wealth is never satisfied with his income. This, too, is meaningless.*
>
> Eccl. 5:10

Do I need a plan for setting aside ten percent of what I earn in my allowance or a part-time job to give back to God? How can I do this?

_____

_____

_____

_____

_____

_____

> *Go to the ant. . . . Consider its ways and be wise!*
> *It has no commander, no overseer or ruler, yet it*

stores its provisions in summer and gathers its food at the harvest.

Prov. 6:6–8

It has been said that tithing is an antidote or prevention for materialism and greed. How does this work?

_____

_____

_____

_____

_____

_____

No one can serve two masters. . . . You cannot serve both God and money.

Matt. 6:24

In Malachi 3:8, God tells His people they are robbing Him by not giving all of their tithes and offerings to Him. Why would the God who created the universe and owns everything be concerned about us "robbing" Him?

_____

_____

_____

_____

_____

_____

*Will a man rob God? Yet you rob me? But you ask,
"How do we rob you?" In tithes and offerings.*

Mal. 3:8

Week 3

How Much of My Time Belongs to God?

SCRIPTURE FOR REFLECTION

Sow your seed in the morning and do not be idle in the evening, for you do not know whether morning or evening sowing will succeed, or whether both of them alike will be good. . . . So, remove vexation from your heart and put away pain from your body, because childhood and the prime of life are fleeting.

Eccl. 11:6; 10 NASB

God gives each of us the same twenty-four hours in every day. Some of use our time wisely, while others squander theirs. Does God care—is "time" something for which we must also answer? Why?

What we do with our time generally parallels what we do with our money. Wherever we put both is where our hearts are. Must tithing come before we buy the things we want and need? Does helping others qualify as tithing? If we use our time to help a friend or neighbor, does God consider this tithing?

Solomon reminds us time and again in both the book of Proverbs and in Ecclesiastes how empty our lives can be when we focus on the wrong things. What really counts? The habits we acquire now will most likely follow us into the rest of our lives unless we choose to change them. God can help us overcome selfishness or laziness in the way we spend our time. Have you thought about how to honor God with your time? Are you honest with God in your tithing?

QUESTIONS TO THINK ABOUT AND JOURNAL ON THIS WEEK

Do I see my time as belonging to God? Am I energetic and productive?

_____

_____

_____

_____

_____

_____

The sluggard craves and gets nothing, but the desires of the diligent are fully satisfied.

Prov. 13:4

In what way have I had the opportunity to help someone recently? What did I do? When I help and assist others, do I consider this a wonderful way to use my time?

_____

_____

_____

_____

_____

_____

_____

_____

*In everything I did, I showed you that by this
kind of hard work we must help the weak,
remembering the words the Lord Jesus himself
said: "It is more blessed to give than to receive."*

Acts 20:35

Do I have goals for my life—short-term and long-term? What are
three personal goals I have for the next five years? Have I asked God
if He thinks these are the best and right goals for me?

_____

_____

_____

_____

_____

_____

_____

*What you decide on will be done and light will
shine on your ways.*

Job 22:28

What are three spiritual goals (aims for my relationship with God or service to others) I have for my life? Have I prayed about these?

_____

_____

_____

_____

_____

_____

_____

For this very reason, make every effort to add to your faith, goodness; and to goodness, knowledge; and to knowledge, self-control; and to self-control, perseverance; and to perseverance, godliness; and to godliness, brotherly kindness; and to brotherly kindness, love.

2 Peter 1:5

Have I had to make a choice recently between doing something I really wanted to do and something I knew I needed to do, like a chore at home? What did I do? Did I ask God to help me do what is right?

_____

_____

_____

_____

_____

_____

*The world and its desires pass away, but the man
who does the will of God lives forever.*

1 John 2:17

What is the one habit affecting my priorities or goals that I most
want to change? Am I willing to ask God to lead me in setting my
priorities right?

_____

_____

_____

_____

_____

_____

*Rid yourselves of all the offenses you have com-
mitted and get a new heart and a new spirit.*

Ezek. 18:31

Look at Ecclesiastes 11:1 on the next page. What did Solomon
mean by that verse?

_____

_____

_____

_____

_____

_____

Cast your bread upon the waters, for after many days you will find it again.

Eccl. 11:1

Week 4

Does God Expect
Me to Witness?

SCRIPTURE FOR REFLECTION

You did not choose me, but I chose you and appointed you to go and bear fruit—fruit that will last. Then the Father will give you whatever you ask in my name. This is my command: love each other.

Although Jesus is talking to his chosen disciples in the verses above, through his Great Commission (see Matt. 28:18–20) he is still making disciples of all who believe. We are, then, the "fruit" of the original disciples. This fruit has the ability to continue reproducing itself as long as the branches it grows upon are joined to the "vine" of Jesus Christ, the living Word. Jesus said that God will prune those branches to make sure they bear the most and the best fruit. Why does God do this to us? So that we can go out into the world and be productive for Him by telling others of His love and His plan of salvation through Jesus Christ.

We are to give God our best, our "first fruits," as the Old Testament says. By making ourselves available for service to Him—in our homes, our churches, our communities and wherever in the world God sends us—we are being good stewards or keepers of what He has given us. What has He given us? Abundant life, brimming with blessings and fruit of every kind. If we don't feel that way, maybe it's because we haven't allowed ourselves to be pruned and fertilized and watered. By loving and serving others, we are increasing God's harvest. Are you ready for that?

QUESTIONS TO THINK ABOUT AND JOURNAL ON THIS WEEK

How did I come to hear about Jesus for the first time? Who "witnessed" to me?

_____

_____

_____

_____

_____

_____

_____

This is good and pleases God our Savior, who wants all men to be saved and to come to a knowledge of the truth.

1 Tim. 2:3,4

Do I belong to a church or attend a youth group? If so, how have I grown? Have I learned to share God with others? Do I believe that the way I live my life is a great part of my own witness?

_____

_____

_____

_____

_____

_____

_____

Grow in the grace and knowledge of our Lord and Savior Jesus Christ.

2 Peter 3:18

Have I had the opportunity to tell someone else about the love of Jesus Christ or what he has done in my life? Do I share the facts of the Gospel, illustrate it from my own experience and invite others to accept Jesus into their lives as Lord and Savior? Why or why not? Do I need to learn how to be a better witness and, if so, will I ask my youth pastor to advise me?

_____

_____

_____

_____

_____

_____

_____

I am not ashamed of the gospel, because it is the power of God for the salvation of everyone who believes.

Rom. 1:16

Have I been "pruned" in any way by God? If so, how? Am I willing to ask Him to examine me and see what needs to go?

_____

_____

_____

_____

_____

_____

_____

_____

Search me, O God, and know my heart; test me and know my anxious thoughts. See if there is any offensive way in me.

Ps. 139:23–24

Have I seen ways to serve God by helping out in my community? What are the needs there?

_____

_____

_____

_____

_____

_____

_____

_____

Serve one another in love. The entire law is summed up in a single command: "Love your neighbor as yourself."

Gal. 5:13b–14

Do I feel that my life is already "bearing fruit" for God? In what ways?

_____

_____

_____

_____

_____

_____

_____

_____

This is to my Father's glory, that you bear much fruit, showing yourselves to be my disciples.

John 15:8

Read John 15:13 on the next page. What does it mean to "lay down" my life for my friends? How can I learn to love others more?

_____

_____

_____

_____

_____

_____

_____

_____

Greater love has no one than this, that he lay down his life for his friends.

John 15:13

Month 11

SERVICE: BEING MY "BROTHER'S KEEPER"

Jesus Christ expects us to "serve" one another in love, as he did when he was among us. That means helping each other in all the ways we can. In this way we become the "salt (seasoning) and the light" of the world, demonstrating the love of Christ to others in need.

We are directed to put the needs of others above our own and to do this with great humility, just as Jesus demonstrated when he washed his disciples' feet. No task is too unimportant if we do it in Jesus' name. We are to be willing to do even the smallest job—without grumbling or wanting a reward. This is how much our Heavenly Father wants us to love one another.

QUESTIONS TO GUIDE THIS MONTH'S DEVOTIONS

- Why is it important for me to use my time and talent to help meet the needs in the world?
- Do I witness my faith in ways that don't "turn others off"?
- What are my own God-given talents and spiritual gifts, and how should I use them?
- How can I know what God may be calling me to do?

Week 1

What Does It Mean to Be "Salt and Light"?

SCRIPTURE FOR REFLECTION

You are the salt of the Earth. But if the salt loses its saltiness, how can it be made salty again? . . . You are the light of the world. A city on a hill cannot be hidden. . . . Let your light shine before men that they may see your good deeds and praise your Father in heaven.

Matt. 5:13a–14; 16

We are to let our "light" shine for everyone to see. Perhaps we remember singing "This Little Light of Mine" when we were little, but as a teenager, in what ways do we reach out with our time and talents to help others?

Just as salt seasons food and gives it better flavor, Jesus wants us to help make the world better and more "flavorful" for others. Can you visit someone who is sick or "shut-in"? How about just looking after a little brother or sister or assisting an elderly neighbor with yard care, housework or grocery shopping? Do you make a point of being extra kind and encouraging to those who are down on their luck, unhappy or going through a rough time? All are "missionary" work. Service work—your "mission field"—is right where you live, work or go to school. List the people you know who need Jesus Christ.

Pray for them regularly, asking God to give you opportunities to talk about His love with them. In these ways your light shines. Jesus wants us to be like that candle—one simple light that, when joined with others like it, forms a giant beacon to point the way to him. Just a simple light that makes a difference in our corner of the world, whether we are joined by other lights or not. Being a "light" glorifies God and is a powerful witness to the world. Does your life demonstrate that you know God?

QUESTIONS TO THINK ABOUT AND JOURNAL ON THIS WEEK

Is it easy for people to tell I am a Christian by my "light"—my actions or attitude? Why or why not?

_____

_____

_____

_____

_____

_____

_____

By this all men will know that you are my disciples, if you love one another.

John 13:35

Look again at Matthew 5:14–16. Do I struggle with Christ's statement that I am to be the "light of the world" and a "city on a hill"?
Does that mean I have to draw attention to myself or witness every
time I help someone? Can I still be salt and light if I serve quietly?

_____

_____

_____

_____

_____

_____

_____

_____

> *You are the light of the world. A city on a hill*
> *cannot be hidden. Neither do people light a*
> *lamp and put it under a bowl. . . . In the same*
> *way, let your light shine before men.*
>
> Matt. 5:14–15a; 16a

What godly person do I most admire? What is it about that person's
"light" that draws me to him or her?

_____

_____

_____

_____

_____

_____

_____

*Be devoted to one another in brotherly love.
Honor one another above yourselves.*

Rom. 12:10

Have I ever been involved with a service project to help someone or an organization in my community or anywhere? If so, what did I gain or learn from it? What did others learn from my simple, straight-forward, "let-me-help-you" approach?

_____

_____

_____

_____

_____

_____

_____

*Dear children, let us not love with words or
tongue, but with actions and in truth.*

1 John 3:18

Have I ever been on the receiving end of some help from a church, an individual or a group of Christians when I really needed it? If so, how did that make me want to pass along the help to others—how would I like to give back?

_____

_____

_____

_____

_____

_____

_____

_____

_____

When men are brought low and you say, "Lift them up!" then He will save the downcast.

Job 22:29

What is a disciple? Do I consider myself a disciple of Jesus Christ? Why or why not?

_____

_____

_____

_____

_____

_____

_____

Anyone who does not carry his cross and follow me cannot be my disciple.

Luke 14:27

When I'm helping others, do I tell them of God's love, or do I feel that is forcing the gospel on them?

_____

_____

_____

_____

_____

_____

_____

_____

*If you spend yourselves in behalf of the hungry
and satisfy the needs of the oppressed, then your
light will rise in the darkness, and your light will
become like the noonday.*

Isa. 58:10

Week 2

How Can I Witness Without Being a "Turn-Off"?

SCRIPTURE FOR REFLECTION

Can a blind man lead a blind man? Will they not both fall into a pit? A student is not above his teacher, but everyone who is fully trained will be like his teacher. . . . Why do you call me 'Lord, Lord' and do not do what I say? . . . The one who hears my words and does not put them into practice is like a man who built a house on the ground without a foundation.

Luke 6:39–40; 46; 49

Can we fly a plane from a few textbook lessons on the ground? Hardly. Likewise, we need to have some knowledge of the Scriptures and experience in serving others in order to be effective Christian leaders/servants. We can share our personal testimony of salvation with others at any time because that will never change. Others may well want to hear what Jesus has done for us. But we all must be careful not to come off as being judgmental or "holier than thou" in our relationships, because it can weaken our effectiveness and really turn others off.

Being overly enthusiastic or zealous can also undermine our testimony. Enthusiasm is fine as long as we're not "thumping" others in the head with our Bibles. Misunderstanding biblical

principles can damage our relationships with those we are trying to help. Love and empathy are the greatest gifts of service
we can give. Likewise, we don't have to be Bible scholars to
help or love others. If we take the time to build a proper foundation, then our "house" will stand firm and our witness for
Christ will be meaningful. Do you build bridges of friendships
that can lead to natural opportunities to share the "good news"
about Jesus?

QUESTIONS TO THINK ABOUT
AND JOURNAL ON THIS WEEK

Do I believe I must "prove" the gospel—or create an intellectual
argument—to convince (or impress) others?

_____

_____

_____

_____

_____

_____

_____

*When I came to you, brothers, I did not come
with eloquence or superior wisdom as I pro-
claimed to you the testimony about God. I came
to you in weakness and fear and much trembling
. . . so that your faith might not rest on men's wisdom but on God's power.*

1 Cor. 2:1; 3; 5

Have I ever been turned off by someone's approach to witnessing the Word of God? If so, how did it make me feel, and what did I say or do as a result?

_____

_____

_____

_____

_____

_____

_____

In your hearts set apart Christ as Lord. Always be prepared to give an answer to everyone who asks you to give the reason for the hope that you have. But do this with gentleness and respect.

1 Peter 3:15

If I am ready to witness, what has been the biggest objection others have expressed to me when I have tried to share the gospel with them? Did I try to overcome that objection? What did I learn from that experience?

_____

_____

_____

_____

_____

_____

> *Am I now trying to win the approval of men, or
> of God? Or am I trying to please men? If I were
> still trying to please men, I would not be a ser-
> vant of Christ.*
>
> Gal. 1:10

Have I been persecuted by someone I was trying to reach out to,
even when I didn't deserve it, just because of another Christian's
prior mistake? If so, how did I handle that situation? Would I do it
differently now?

_____

_____

_____

_____

_____

_____

_____

> *Others, like seed sown on rocky places, hear the
> word and at once receive it with joy. But since
> they have no root, they last only a short time.
> When trouble or persecution comes because of
> the word, they quickly fall away.*
>
> Mark 4:16–17

Look at Luke 6:27–36. What is the real reason Jesus says we must
"be merciful" to those who dislike or hurt us?

_____

_____

_____

_____

_____

_____

_____

_____

*But I tell you who hear me: Love your enemies,
do good to those who hate you, bless those who
curse you, pray for those who mistreat you. . . .
Be merciful, just as your Father is merciful.*

Luke 6:27–28; 36

Do I know anyone I consider a Christian hypocrite? Have I ever been
a hypocrite? What problems are caused by such hypocrisy, and what
can I do to repair the damage this may have caused?

_____

_____

_____

_____

_____

_____

_____

*He said to them, "You are the ones who justify
yourselves in the eyes of men, but God knows
your hearts. What is highly valued among men is
detestable in God's sight."*

Luke 16:15

Has anyone I once trusted, and considered a Christian, led me astray in any way? If so, how did I react to that? What did I learn that can help me be more effective in my witnessing to others?

_____

_____

_____

_____

_____

_____

_____

Turn away from godless chatter and the opposing ideas of what is falsely called knowledge, which some have professed and in so doing have wandered from the faith.

1 Tim. 20–21

Week 3

What Are My "Spiritual Gifts," and How Am I to Use Them?

SCRIPTURE FOR REFLECTION

There are different kinds of gifts, but the same Spirit. There are different kinds of service, but the same Lord. . . . Now to each one the manifestation of the Spirit is given for the common good. And in the church, God has appointed first of all apostles, second prophets, third teachers, then workers of miracles, also those having gifts of healing, those able to help others, those with gifts of administration and those speaking in different kinds of tongues.

1 Cor. 12:4–5; 7; 28

Each of us is uniquely "gifted" with an ability and a desire for Christian service in one or more specific areas. The apostle Paul uses the analogy of these various abilities and talents working together in the church as being like the various parts of the human body working together for the benefit of the whole. In fact, the church often is called "the body of Christ." It is the Holy Spirit who assigns these spiritual gifts to believers so we also can build up and encourage each other. Perhaps you already know what your gifts are. If you don't, you can find out. That is one of the purposes of this month's journaling.

In Appendix B on page 319, you will find a Spiritual Gifts Survey that asks you to evaluate yourself in a number of areas to determine your interests and abilities with regard to Christian service. These represent the areas of service for which you will be best suited and will enjoy the most. You may be surprised at what you learn about your gifts, but know that God doesn't make any mistakes in His "appointments." He may even put you to work in an area in which you don't feel very strong so you can gain strength and confidence. Ultimately, if you follow His calling, you will find the best ways to serve others and to help build God's church, whether at home or abroad. Will you listen to His calling?

QUESTIONS TO THINK ABOUT AND JOURNAL ON THIS WEEK

According to the Spiritual Gifts Survey in Appendix B, what are my spiritual gifts? Do any of the results surprise me, or do they conform to what I already believed?

_____

_____

_____

_____

_____

_____

_____

But to each one of us grace has been given as Christ apportioned it. This is why it says: "When he ascended on high, he led captives in his train and gave gifts to men."

Eph. 4:7–8

Have I already been using any of these gifts in service in my church, school or community? If so, how?

_____

_____

_____

_____

_____

_____

_____

_____

Therefore, as we have opportunity, let us do good to all people, especially to those who belong to the family of believers.

Gal. 6:10

If I am not already serving in any of these areas, how can I begin doing so?

_____

_____

_____

_____

_____

_____

_____

Be diligent in these matters; give yourself wholly
to them so that everyone may see your progress.

1 Tim. 4:15

In looking over the results of the Spiritual Gifts Survey, would I say
that God is preparing me to be an evangelist, a teacher, pastor,
apostle or prophet—or none of these? How do I know for sure?

_____

_____

_____

_____

_____

_____

_____

_____

And He Himself gave some to be apostles, some
prophets, some evangelists, and some pastors
and teachers, for the equipping of the saints for
the work of the ministry.

Eph. 4:11–12

Do I believe that the spiritual gifts God has given me are inten-
tional—that He has specific plans for equipping me for service to
benefit His kingdom?

_____

_____

_____

_____

_____

_____

_____

_____

_____

_____

"Ah, Sovereign Lord," I said, "I do not know how to speak; I am only a child." But the Lord said to me, "Do not say, 'I am only a child.' You must go to everyone I send you to and say whatever I command you. Do not be afraid of them, for I am with you and will rescue you," declares the Lord. Then the Lord reached out His hand and touched my mouth and said to me, "Now, I have put my words in your mouth."

Jer. 1:6–9

Why do I think some people get "burned out" in Christian service? How can I avoid this myself?

_____

_____

_____

_____

_____

_____

_____

_____

The eye cannot say to the hand, "I don't need you!" and the head cannot say to the feet, "I don't need you!" . . . If one part suffers, every part suffers with it; if one part is honored, every part rejoices with it.

1 Cor. 12:21; 26

Look at 1 Corinthians 12:12–26. How do Christians sometimes forget about this teaching of Paul and actually hurt the work of the church?

_____

_____

_____

_____

_____

_____

_____

The body is a unit, though it is made up of many parts. . . . If the whole body were an eye, where would the sense of hearing be? If the whole body were an ear, where would the sense of smell be? But, in fact, God arranged the parts in the body, every one of them, just as He wanted them to be.

1 Cor. 12:12; 17–18

Week 4

Helping Others: How Will I Know What God Wants Me to Do?

SCRIPTURE FOR REFLECTION

"For I know the plans that I have for you,"
declares the Lord, "plans to prosper you and not
to harm you, plans to give you hope and a
future. Then you will call upon Me and come
and pray to Me, and I will listen to you. You will
seek Me and find Me when you seek Me with all
your heart."

Jer. 29:11–13

God has specific plans for blessing us and equipping us for service in His kingdom. We can choose to find our own way of serving, but we would be wise to trust in God's call. How are we to know what God has in mind for us? How will He call us to serve Him? Will He put us in a place far away, or will He use us closer to home? The answers to these questions are not difficult to answer. First, He asks us to seek Him through prayer and a willing heart. When He answers, He may also ask us to go through a period of testing while He strengthens us. This is what happened to Jesus as he waited in the wilderness before he started his ministry. It also happened to the apostle Paul after his dramatic meeting with the risen Lord and his conversion on the road to Damascus. Our calling may not be so dramatic, but we will know it is authentic if we pray earnestly for God's will.

Once we are "appointed" by God, He will give us opportunities to learn how to serve effectively. He will ask us to "bloom where we are planted," even though it may appear that He has placed us in a dry desert. God can grow us anywhere He wants. He makes "streams in the desert" and greatly multiplies our efforts when we serve with all our hearts. No matter how little or big the task, when God gives it, we will know it is important. To use the body analogy that Paul used, we may think the toe is an unworthy or useless part of the body until we realize that, without toes, the foot can't balance and we can't walk. Have you prayed yet for God's direction in your life? Are you ready to begin seeking it? He will call us when He is ready. It may be months or years from now. That's okay.

QUESTIONS TO THINK ABOUT
AND JOURNAL ON THIS WEEK

Now that I have a better idea of my spiritual gifts, how will I pray for God to use them as I seek His will for my life?

Ask and it will be given to you; seek and you will find; knock and the door will be opened to you.

Matt. 7:7

Have I ever felt that God may be calling me or urging me to do something? If so, did I answer? What happened?

_____

_____

_____

_____

_____

_____

Then the Lord called Samuel. . . . Now Samuel did not yet know the Lord; the Word of the Lord had not yet been revealed to him. . . . So Eli told Samuel, "Go and lie down, and if He calls you, say, 'Speak, Lord, for your servant is listening.'"

1 Sam. 3:4; 7; 9

Do I know of a situation where God used someone to confirm what He wanted another person, or me, to do? If so, what happened?

_____

_____

_____

_____

_____

_____

_____

_____

_____

I thank my God always concerning you, for the grace of God, which was given you in Christ Jesus, that in everything you were enriched in him . . . even as the testimony concerning Christ was confirmed in you.

1 Cor. 1:4–6 NASB

Suppose I felt God calling me to do something I didn't want to do or I thought would be too hard. Would I have a heart-to-heart with God about it? Why or why not?

_____

_____

_____

_____

_____

_____

_____

He gives strength to the weary and increases the power of the weak.

Isa. 40:29

What can I learn from my willingness to serve God by doing things for others?

_____

_____

_____

_____

_____

_____

_____

> *His master replied, "Well done, good and faithful servant! You have been faithful with a few things; I will put you in charge of many things. Come and share your master's happiness!"*
>
> Matt. 25:21

Sharing my testimony, my personal relationship with Jesus Christ, is a powerful and effective way to witness. What was my life like before I met Jesus Christ as Lord and Savior, and what is it like now after receiving him?

_____

_____

_____

_____

_____

_____

_____

Be transformed by the renewing of your mind.
Then you will be able to test and approve what
God's will is—His good, pleasing and perfect
will.

Rom. 12:2

Look at Jeremiah 29:13–14. God used the prophet Jeremiah to
speak for Him to the Israelites and tell them that He would forgive
their disobedience and bless them once more if they turned back to
Him. Have I felt confused over how to obey God? Do I need to ask
for forgiveness and to get on track with Him so He can bless me and
reveal His plans to me? If so, here is my prayer:

_____

_____

_____

_____

_____

_____

_____

"You will seek Me and find Me when you seek
Me with all your heart. I will be found by you,"
declares the Lord, "and will bring you back from
captivity."

Jer. 29:13–14a

Month 12

COURAGE: WALKING WITH GOD

Are you walking with God? As we continue to look to Him for strength and wisdom, He will give us the courage and grace both to meet the challenges that come our way and to encourage others by setting an example of our own faith. God promises us the "riches of His glory" if we believe in Him—if we live our lives according to the laws He set out so we might experience the abundance of His love.

QUESTIONS TO GUIDE THIS MONTH'S DEVOTIONS

- How does God use difficult experiences to strengthen my faith?
- How can I use my life and testimony to encourage and build up others?
- How does God continue teaching me and showing me His will?
- How does God hold me accountable for the choices I make?

Week 1

Why Does God "Test" Me?

SCRIPTURE FOR REFLECTION

Consider it pure joy, my brothers, whenever you face trials of many kinds, because you know that the testing of your faith develops perseverance. Perseverance must finish its work so that you may be mature and complete, not lacking anything.

James 1:1–4

Is a trial—something really big and difficult—to deal with on our own? Or is it a series of things that we think are small enough for us to handle—until one day we realize we can't? It's both, isn't it? Struggles in life are unavoidable. We're all going to have them. The sooner we realize that we don't have to handle everything, the sooner we will be able to find relief and insight and renewed faith by letting God be God. That does not make us cowards or losers. It makes us human. Our God is an almighty God. What is impossible with us is always possible with Him. Have you been trying to take care of yourself? Have you failed to use all the strength available to you, like the boy who struggled to pick up a large rock? He kept going back to his dad and telling him he couldn't do it. His dad asked each time, "Are you using all your strength?" The boy replied that he was. "But did you ask me to help?" asked his father. Sometimes God sends His strength in the form of other caring people.

God won't take our problems away or take us away from them. There is only one way we can go, and that is straight through them. We can't grow and learn any other way. As we overcome each obstacle in our path, we gain faith and ability to help others who are also struggling. "The battle is the Lord's." We have only to ask for His help. What trials are you facing? Have you used *all* your strength?

QUESTIONS TO THINK ABOUT AND JOURNAL ON THIS WEEK

Am I the kind of person who likes to be self-sufficient? If so, why do I think it is hard for me to let others or God help me?

_____

_____

_____

_____

_____

_____

_____

The Lord is good, a refuge in times of trouble. He cares for those who trust in Him.

Nahum 1:7

What is the most difficult challenge I have faced in my life so far?
Have I made it through, or am I still overcoming it? How has it
changed me?

_____

_____

_____

_____

_____

_____

_____

> *Be strong and take heart, all you who hope in
> the Lord.*
>
> Ps. 31:24

What did I do (or am I still doing) in overcoming my challenge that
was (or is) the biggest help to me? For example, do I pray or ask God
for guidance? Do I ask others to support me?

_____

_____

_____

_____

_____

_____

_____

"Have faith in God," Jesus answered. "I tell you the truth, if anyone says to this mountain, 'go throw yourself into the sea,' and does not doubt in his heart but believes that what he says will happen, it will be done for him."

Mark 11:22–23

How would I be willing to help someone who was facing a difficult challenge similar to one I'd faced? What would I do to help—for example, would I talk with this person, or pray for or with this person?

_____

_____

_____

_____

_____

_____

_____

For just as the sufferings of Christ flow over into our lives, so also through Christ our comfort overflows.

2 Cor. 1:5

What would I do if I wanted to help someone, but that person was too shy or stubborn to let me help?

_____

_____

_____

_____
_____
_____
_____
_____

*Let us not become weary in doing good, for at the
proper time we will reap a harvest if we do not
give up.*

Gal. 6:9

What selfish goal, desire or temptation has drawn me away from
God, and what must I do to return to His grace?

_____
_____
_____
_____
_____
_____
_____

*I press on toward the goal to win the prize for
which God has called me heavenward in Christ
Jesus. All of us who are mature should take such
a view of things. And if on some point you think
differently, that, too, God will make clear to you.*

Phil. 3:14–15

Look at James 1:5–8. How does my faith influence or "allow" the help I receive from God?

_____

_____

_____

_____

_____

_____

If any of you lacks wisdom, he should ask God, who gives generously to all without finding fault, and it will be given to him. But when he asks, he must believe and not doubt, because he who doubts is like a wave of the sea, blown and tossed by the wind.

James 1:5–6

Week 2

Does God Always Expect Me to Be an Example to Others?

SCRIPTURE FOR REFLECTION

I have been reminded of your sincere faith, which first lived in your grandmother Lois and in your mother Eunice and, I am persuaded, now lives in you also. For this reason I remind you to fan into flame the gift of God, which is in you through the laying on of my hands. For God did not give us a spirit of timidity, but a spirit of power, of love and of self-discipline. So do not be ashamed to testify about our Lord.

2 Tim. 1:5–8a

The New Testament records two letters the apostle Paul wrote to his young friend and pupil, Timothy. They contain some of the most memorable language in Scripture. His letters to Timothy are more personal and fatherly than any others. Here, Paul didn't have to correct quarreling church congregations, but he simply wanted to encourage and instruct young Timothy, to whom he referred as a "dear son" in his own ministry. Paul was passing the torch. What he wrote in this second letter to Timothy is all the more meaningful because these were the last words he is known to have written. He was to be put to death for his faith not long after.

As the next generation to come into adulthood, today's teens are preparing to take the torch of those who have gone before—a torch that has been passed from Jesus Christ through the great apostles all the way down to us. Do you feel ready to take up the challenge of continuing to share God's love and hope with the world? How will you do that? Paul tells Timothy to "guard the good deposit that was entrusted to you" (2 Tim. 1:14) with the help of the Holy Spirit. That same Spirit is in us, if we have made the commitment to live for Christ. Others will be watching us. Are you going to show them the right example? With God's help, we can have that kind of courage and resolve.

QUESTIONS TO THINK ABOUT
AND JOURNAL ON THIS WEEK

What is the hardest part of witnessing or sharing my faith with others? Why?

_____

_____

_____

_____

_____

_____

_____

I am not ashamed, because I know whom I have believed, and I know he is able to guard what I have entrusted to him for that day.

2 Tim. 1:12

Has anyone ever made fun of me for being a Christian? How did I react? Did it change the way I feel about God?

_____

_____

_____

_____

_____

_____

_____

> *Blessed are you when people insult you, perse-cute you and falsely say all kinds of evil against you because of me. Rejoice and be glad, because great is your reward in heaven, for in the same way they persecuted the prophets who were before you.*
>
> Matt. 5:11

What is my own salvation testimony? How did I come to accept Jesus as my personal Savior? (Or am I still waiting to make that decision, and if so, why?)

_____

_____

_____

_____

_____

_____

_____

Anyone who believes in the Son of God has this testimony in his heart. . . . And this is the testimony: God has given us eternal life, and this life is in His Son.

1 John 5:10a–11

If someone has shared the gospel message with me one-on-one, what impressed me most about his or her witnessing?

_____

_____

_____

_____

_____

_____

_____

Blessed are the pure in heart, for they will see God.

Matt. 5:8

How would I rate the example I set for others on a scale of 1–10, with 1 being shy and lacking confidence and 10 being a dedicated disciple of Christ? How do I think others would rate me? Why?

_____

_____

_____

_____

_____

_____

_____

Each one has used whatever gift he has received to serve others, faithfully administering God's grace in its various forms.

1 Peter 4:10

Am I a Christian 24/7 (even when no one is looking)? Why or why not?

_____

_____

_____

_____

_____

_____

_____

Speak and act as those who are going to be judged by the law that gives freedom.

James 2:12

Read 2 Timothy 1:4, 7 and 8. Does it sound as if Timothy had been afraid or lacking in confidence without Paul at his side? How does it help me to know that even the "saints" of the early church sometimes were lacking in courage?

_____

_____

_____

_____

_____

_____

_____

_____

Recalling your tears, I long to see you so that I may be filled with joy. . . . So do not be ashamed to testify about our Lord, or ashamed of me his prisoner.

2 Tim. 1:4; 8a

Week 3

How Can I Keep My Faith at the Center of My Life— No Matter What?

SCRIPTURE FOR REFLECTION

So then, just as you received Christ Jesus as Lord, continue to live in him, rooted and built up in him, strengthened in the faith as you were taught, and overflowing with thankfulness.

Col. 2:6–7

It's one thing to live in the newfound joy that follows accepting Jesus as our personal Lord and Savior, but will we stay in that place when the problems of life come calling? Will we remind ourselves that it is precisely in times of trial when we need to call on God's grace to give us strength and courage to stand up to the challenges?

Luckily, we are not given a limited supply of faith from which to draw our whole lives. God expects us to grow our faith, one day at a time, one challenge at a time. Faith allows us to know we can and will persevere. Faith causes us to meet the challenge—which causes us to have more faith, which causes us to act some more . . . and on and on it goes. Each time we stand up for what we believe and do the right thing, we add a growth ring to that tree of ours that Psalm 1:3 says is "firmly planted by streams of water." If we want to grow, we must get up the courage to get out of our little pots and plant ourselves firmly in the living Word of God. Then our roots can spread, and we will stand tall and unafraid. Often, youth knows no fear. That is why God has chosen teenagers many times to carry His message out into the world. What may God be asking you to do?

QUESTIONS TO THINK ABOUT AND JOURNAL ON THIS WEEK

Would I say I am "planted" in the firm soil of God's Word, or am I still in the "pot," waiting to get my roots into the ground?

_____

_____

_____

_____

_____

_____

He is like a tree planted by streams of water, which yields its fruit in season and whose leaf does not wither. Whatever he does prospers.

Ps. 1:3

Have I experienced an emotional low following a high or a "mountaintop" experience? If so, how did it affect my faith?

_____

_____

_____

_____

_____

_____

_____

> *There is a time for everything, and a season for every activity under heaven . . . a time to weep and a time to laugh, a time to mourn and a time to dance.*
>
> Eccl. 3:4

Have I found that I have the ability to "bend in the wind" and get right back up when the world is pushing me around? Why or why not?

_____

_____

_____

_____

_____

_____

_____

The righteous will flourish like a palm tree, they will grow like a cedar of Lebanon; planted in the house of the Lord, they will flourish in the courts of our God.

Ps. 92:12–13

Do I feel that I lack confidence because of my age, or do I have an advantage in my youthful faith? Am I sometimes overconfident?

_____

_____

_____

_____

_____

_____

_____

For you have been my hope, O Sovereign Lord, my confidence since my youth.

Ps. 71:5

What event in my life so far has been responsible for stretching my faith the most?

_____

_____

_____

_____

_____

_____

_____

*Against all hope, Abraham in hope believed and
so became the father of many nations. . . . Yet he
did not waver through unbelief regarding the
promise of God, but was strengthened in his
faith and gave glory to God, being fully persuaded that God had power to do what He had
promised.*

Rom. 4:18; 20–21

Have I learned to actually thank God for the tough times? How do
these times make me stronger?

_____

_____

_____

_____

_____

_____

_____

_____

*But we also rejoice in our sufferings, because we
know that suffering produces perseverance, perseverance character, and character hope.*

Rom. 5:3–4

Look at Colossians 2:8 and 23. Am I sometimes confused by other religions or ideas that would have me put myself instead of God at the center of everything or follow certain strict human rules? How does believing this way hurt my faith in God?

_____

_____

_____

_____

_____

_____

_____

> *See to it that no one takes you captive through hollow and deceptive philosophy, which depends on human tradition and the basic principles of this world rather than on Christ. . . . Such regulations indeed have an appearance of wisdom, but they lack any value in restraining sensual indulgence.*
>
> Col. 2:8; 23

Week 4

How Will My Life Glorify God?

SCRIPTURE FOR REFLECTION

His divine power has given us everything we need for life and godliness through our knowledge of him who called us by his own glory and goodness. Through these he has given us his very great and precious promises, so that through them you may participate in the divine nature and escape the corruptness in the world caused by evil desires.

2 Peter 1:3–4

As God spoke the world into existence, so He speaks our destinies. When we come to understand that God (Father, Son and Holy Spirit) calls us to be all that we can be—to do our "utmost for His highest," as the Scottish preacher Oswald Chambers said—then we are ready to make ourselves available to be shaped and molded in His image. God wants to perfect us (the technical term is "sanctify") over the course of our walk with Him.

What does all this mean for us? *I'm only a teenager,* you may believe. Well, for starters, it means you have a long, wonderful road ahead of you. You have much to learn still, but you have the same gift of grace, the same active faith that any saint who has gone before you has had. We are connected through all those who have gone before to the same God. Awesome!

What will you do with your faith? How will you live your life in order to glorify and reflect God? Those "precious promises" of old give us all the strength and assurance we need. We know the road will be bumpy in places, but God will be with us. Why would we not want to keep our eyes on Him, knowing how powerful and gracious He is? Just anticipating what He will do with our lives can be exciting! "I have summoned you by name; you are Mine!" (Isa. 43:1). God sent His son to save our lives, and assured us, just as Paul knew, that "I can do everything through him who gives me strength" (Phil. 4:13). It will never get any better than that.

QUESTIONS TO THINK ABOUT
AND JOURNAL ON THIS WEEK

Do I feel more like a son or daughter of God—a "fellow heir" with Christ—now than I did when I began this devotional journal? Why or why not?

_____

_____

_____

_____

_____

_____

_____

_____

In love, He destined us to be adopted as His sons through Jesus Christ, in accordance with His pleasure and will—to the praise of His glorious

*grace, which He has freely given us in One He
loves.*

Eph. 1:5–6

If I still struggle to accept that I am God's chosen ambassador or
worker here on Earth, what do I see as the real obstacle to my
belief? How can I overcome it? Am I willing to talk to a pastor or
other counselor?

_____

_____

_____

_____

_____

_____

_____

*For we are God's fellow workers; you are God's
field, God's building.*

1 Cor. 3:9

Am I ready to face someone who may challenge my beliefs? What
will I say to that person?

_____

_____

_____

_____

_____

_____

_____

> *But in your hearts, set apart Christ as Lord.*
> *Always be prepared to give an answer to every-*
> *one who asks you to give the reason for the hope*
> *that you have. But do this with gentleness and*
> *respect, keeping a clear conscience, so that those*
> *who speak maliciously against your good behav-*
> *ior in Christ may be ashamed of their slander.*
>
> 1 Peter 3:15–16

Am I prepared to let God's path take me wherever He wants to carry me, even when I may not understand? Why or why not?

_____

_____

_____

_____

_____

_____

_____

> *The path of the righteous is like the first gleam of*
> *dawn, shining ever brighter till the full light of*
> *day.*
>
> Prov. 4:18

Am I still being tempted or troubled by some area in my life, such as drugs or alcohol, sexual sin, greed, pride, laziness? If so, how can

I use what I have learned in this journal to strengthen me in those areas? Do I need to seek help from someone?

_____

_____

_____

_____

_____

_____

Is any one of you in trouble? He should pray. . . .
If he has sinned, he will be forgiven. Therefore
confess your sins to each other and pray for each
other so that you might be healed. The prayer of
a righteous man is powerful and effective.

James 5:13a; 15b–16

What is the one thing I most want to accomplish for God through my own Christian testimony or walk in the near future? How will I do it?

_____

_____

_____

_____

_____

_____

_____

He who began a good work in you will carry it on to completion until the day of Christ Jesus.

Phil. 1:6

Look at 2 Peter 1:5–11. What does Peter's statement: "Be all the more eager to make your calling and election sure" mean? How can I do this for myself?

_____

_____

_____

_____

_____

_____

_____

_____

For if you possess these qualities in increasing measure, they will keep you from being ineffective and unproductive in your knowledge of our Lord Jesus Christ.

2 Peter 1:8

Epilogue

We're pleased to have had the opportunity to help you further your knowledge of and relationship with God through these twelve months of devotion and prayer. There are so many ways that "real life" can make you feel confused and insecure, and leave you wondering what is right (versus best) and what is important (versus urgent). This is all the more reason to ask God to be with you on each and every step you take. Continue to take the time—make the time—to talk with God on a daily basis, so you might develop a deep and growing personal relationship with your Heavenly Father. Ask God to make His truths known to you, then thank Him for His faithfulness and goodness toward you.

Always remember that God is the source of direction, wisdom, strength, peace and joy. When we faithfully meet Him in Bible study and prayer, our priorities shift, and we live our lives with more joy and abundance. Let God be at the center of your life. Courageously live your Christianity. Review these specific Scriptures from time to time to remind yourself about what is really important:

Seeking God through prayer: Matt. 7:7; Phil. 4:6–7
Knowing God's Word: Ps. 19:7–8; 2 Tim. 3:14–17
Fellowship and worship with other believers: Heb. 10:24–25

Repentance and acceptance of Jesus: Acts 3:19; John 1:12
Love for others: John 13:34–35; 1 Cor. 13:4–7
Power of the Holy Spirit: Acts 1:18; Rom. 8:26
Evidence of the Spirit-filled life: Gal. 5:22–23;
    1 John 4:12–13
Identification with Jesus Christ: Rom. 6:3–4; Gal. 2:20
Victory over sin and death: Rom. 8:37–39; 1 Cor. 15:54–57
Witnessing for Christ: Matt. 4:19; Matt. 28:19–20

After working through this devotional journal, you will have identified ways in which you can make your walk with God and your witness to others much stronger. God gives us the power and ability to speak about His continuing work in us and to show others by our example that we are committed Christians. They will see that you are "walking in the Spirit" and that your life is fruitful because of it. God will continue to bless and grow you as you keep your focus on Him in the years ahead. That will be our prayer for you.

Bettie, Jennifer and Debbie

Abbreviations for Books of the Bible

Old Testament

		New Testament	

Old Testament		New Testament	
1 Chronicles	1 Chron.	Colossians	Col.
2 Chronicles	2 Chron.	1 Corinthians	1 Cor.
Deuteronomy	Deut.	2 Corinthians	2 Cor.
Ecclesiastes	Eccl.	Ephesians	Eph.
Exodus	Exod.	Galatians	Gal.
Ezekiel	Ezek.	Hebrews	Heb.
Genesis	Gen.	Matthew	Matt.
Isaiah	Isa.	Philippians	Phil.
Jeremiah	Jer.	Revelation	Rev.
Joshua	Josh.	Romans	Rom.
Leviticus	Lev.	1 Thessalonians	1 Thess.
Malachi	Mal.	2 Thessalonians	2 Thess.
Numbers	Num.	1 Timothy	1 Tim.
Proverbs	Prov.	2 Timothy	2 Tim.
Psalms	Ps.		
1 Samuel	1 Sam.		
2 Samuel	2 Sam.		

Appendix A: Simple Prayers for Christian Living

The Lord's Prayer

Our Father who art in heaven,
Hallowed be thy name;
Thy kingdom come.
Thy will be done on Earth
as it is in heaven.
Give us this day our daily bread.
And forgive us our debts,
As we forgive our debtors.
And lead us not into temptation,
But deliver us from evil:
For thine is the kingdom,
and the power, and the glory, forever. Amen.

The Serenity Prayer

God grant me the serenity
to accept the things I cannot change,
courage to change the things I can
and the wisdom to know the difference.

A Prayer for Salvation

Dear Father, I realize that I am a sinner
And that I cannot change anything I have done.
But You can give me a new life, Lord,
if I give my old one to You.
Forgive me for my sins and accept me into Your holy family.
I know that You sent Your only son, Jesus,
into the world to die for my sins. I believe that he is
the way, the truth and the life,
and I accept him now as my personal Savior.
Thank You, Lord, for hearing my prayer
and for giving me eternal life.

A Prayer of Thanksgiving

Heavenly Father, I offer You praise and thanks
for who You are and for all that You have done.
You have created this wondrous universe
and all things are under Your control.
You made me, Father, just the way You wanted me,
and You put in me your Holy Spirit
so that I could be more like You.
Your blessings are too numerous to count.
You have always been there with what I need
just when I need it.
I know I can bring any problem, no matter how small, to You
and You will help me work it out according to Your will.
I promise to love and serve You all of my life
because You want what is best for me.
May I always seek You first, above all else.

A Prayer for Healing

Dear God, today I am in need of Your healing touch.
You know just what ails me, even before I speak it.
You understand all that I am feeling because
You have suffered all things in the form of Jesus Christ.
Take my pain, Lord, and use it to show me Your truth.
If it is Your will, heal me and remove my pain.
If You have some purpose for this affliction,
Show me what it is, Lord.
"I can do all things through Him who gives me strength."
If You wish to make me stronger through this pain, Lord,
then so be it.
Give me the courage to withstand it
and the grace to be an example to others.
Forgive me if I sin in my pain and selfishness.
Show me that all things are working for good through You.

A Prayer for Courage

Father, today I need Your strength
to help me get through the challenges I am facing.
I know that You have not given me a spirit of fear,
but of courage and a sound mind.
Yet, I am frightened when I think of what I must do.
Strengthen me, Lord, and help me to shed my fear.
You are the God who delivered Daniel from the lion's den,
And I know You can deliver me if You choose to.
Father, show me how to stand tall
and to be bold in the midst of this situation.
Help me to do whatever I must to bring glory
and honor to Your name.
If you choose not to deliver me, then stand beside me
and help me to get through this.
Thank you, God, for being my help and my strength.

A Prayer for Peace

God, as I look around me I see people absorbed in conflicts.
The world is in turmoil because too many people
do not know You.
Open their eyes, Lord, and show them that You have the answer.
Send your Holy Spirit to convict and change hearts.
Only then will people understand what is truly important.
Father, help me to do my part in sharing Your truth
with others who do not know You.
Give me courage and wisdom
to know how to set a godly example for others around me to see.
As we all long for peace in the world, Father,
so we also long for peace in our hearts.
Touch the hearts of those who are suffering and oppressed,
Especially help those who are too weak to help themselves.
And, Father, give us the grace to forgive the oppressors.
You sent Your Son into the world to be the Prince of Peace.
May the world know that peace.

A Prayer for Grace

Dear God, You know what I am facing today.
I cannot face it on my own. Give me Your grace
and send Your peace to comfort me in my confusion.
You have said that Your grace is sufficient
and that Your strength is made perfect in our weakness.
Father, I feel so weak today.
You know exactly what I need even before I ask.
My prayer is that You will give me a calm spirit
and a clear mind so that I can see which way to go.
Be my rock, Lord, and let me hold onto You.
Your Word is a lamp for my feet and a light to my path.
Guide me in Your truth.

A Prayer for Wisdom

Lord, I am struggling today with a decision I must make.
There are so many ways I could go.
Is there a best way, Lord? If so, will You show me?
You have said that You will make our paths straight
if we commit all our ways to You.
I am laying this decision at Your feet, Father.
Open my eyes to Your truth. Send Your Holy Spirit to guide me.
Help me to accept the decision I make
and to do everything in my strength to make it right.
If You close a door, I know You will open a window.
Your ways are higher than my ways.
Give me Your peace and clear vision to see the road ahead.
Thank You for being my strength.

A Prayer for the Needs of Others

Dear Father, someone I love is in need of Your touch today.
Please bring Your grace to my friends.
Help them to wait before You and to seek Your strength
instead of trying to do it by themselves.
You can provide for their needs because You are God.
If it is Your will, You can heal or You can change circumstances.
Show them that you are in control and give them Your peace.
Help them to have the courage to know what they can change
and the serenity to know what they can't.
Give them a deeper knowledge of who You are through this struggle.
Strengthen their trust and help them to glorify You in all their trials.

Appendix B:
Spiritual Gifts Survey

Sharing our time and talents with others is one of the many ways we serve God. While some teens know exactly how to best do this, others would like to better know how they can be of service in ways that are both fun and natural for them. How about you—do you know how you can best contribute your time and talent in serving your church or community? The following survey can help you discover more about your own special interests and strengths as they relate to Christian service.

In the following survey you'll find forty questions designed to help you identify your own special talents, strengths, passions—your spiritual or God-given gifts—as they relate to serving others and bringing glory and honor to God. You'll also find a chart for scoring the answers to your survey, a chart for explaining each spiritual gift and space for ranking your highest scores. Read the directions and then follow each step. If you aren't sure about how a particular statement applies to you (or don't understand the statement), you may wish to ask your mom or dad, or a youth worker in your church. [Special note: You may want to consider making an extra copy or two of this survey before you write on it so you can share a copy with family and friends.]

INSTRUCTIONS

1. Read each of the forty statements on the Spiritual Gifts Survey and rate each one using the following value scale:
   NOT AT ALL = 0   LITTLE = 1   SOME = 2   MUCH = 3

2. Enter your 0–3 rating for each statement on the score sheet.

3. Add up each letter row (straight across) and enter that number in the corresponding "Total" blank. Your scores will range from 0 to 12. For example:

Rows	Value of Answers	Total	Gift
Row A	1: 3 11: 3 21: 2 31: 2	10	PROPHECY

4. You then go to the "Gifts Explained" chart at the end of this section and match your totals to the gifts they represent. For example, if the total of 10 in Row A was one of the highest totals on the score sheet, this would show that you may have the spiritual gift of PROPHECY, followed by a listing of Scripture that supports the importance of sharing this particular gift (shown in the example below).

Row	Gift	Scripture
A:	PROPHECY—to proclaim the truth or Word of God in a way that brings conviction to the hearers.	Acts 15:32; 1 Cor. 13:2; 14:1–3

5. Using the lines below, record your four highest scores. These four will give you a reasonable idea of your strengths and aptitudes for ways you can best share yourself in Christian service.

- _____

- _____

- _____

- _____

SCORING SHEET

Rows	Value of Answers				Total	Gift
Row A	1:	11:	21:	31:	_____	PROPHECY
Row B	2:	12:	22:	32:	_____	SHEPHERDING
Row C	3:	13:	23:	33:	_____	EVANGELISM
Row D	4:	14:	24:	34:	_____	ENCOURAGEMENT
Row E	5:	15:	25:	35:	_____	TEACHING
Row F	6:	16:	26:	36:	_____	GIVING
Row G	7:	17:	27:	37:	_____	INTERCESSION
Row H	8:	18:	28:	38:	_____	MERCY
Row I	9:	19:	29:	39:	_____	ADMINISTRATION
Row J	10:	20:	30:	40:	_____	SERVICE

SPIRITUAL GIFTS SURVEY

Rate each of the following statements using:

NOT AT ALL = 0   LITTLE = 1   SOME = 2   MUCH = 3

1. I enjoy talking to others about God and about being a Christian.

2. I enjoy helping others better understand the Christian faith and helping them to know God personally.

3. I enjoy helping others to recognize God's grace in their lives.

4. I enjoy sharing words of encouragement with those who are feeling discouraged, down or without direction.

5. I like to help others learn how to have a "better life."

6. I am diligent about setting aside some of my allowance earnings to give to God's work.

7. I feel that prayer is important, and I make a point to pray often for others.

8. I enjoy working with those who are in need, especially those who are spiritually "thirsty."

9. I enjoy getting others to help out, rallying together for a good cause.

10. I enjoy being called on to do special jobs.

11. I enjoy telling others about the Word of God and helping them to gain a better understanding of what it means for their lives.

12. I feel led to help others who are struggling with faith or are in a crisis.

13. I share my own journey of faith gladly and thoughtfully with other people.

14. I like to encourage those who feel down or discouraged in order to help them renew their hope.

15. I enjoy sharing the Bible with children and adults.

16. I like sharing my money and donating things that further God's word.

17. I often find myself praying, even in the middle of doing other things.

18. I like visiting or sharing with those who are "shut-in"—such as the elderly or incarcerated.

19. I am good at organizing and managing people and projects.

20. I enjoy routine.

21. I enjoy talking about the great truths of God.

22. I like being part of a group and supporting them in their successes and failures.

23. I love sharing with others the joy of my personal walk with Jesus.

24. I am good at helping others—even those who say they do not believe in Jesus—to think about God and His presence in all things.

25. I am good at explaining even difficult things to others.

26. I love to give of myself so that God's work can be extended and helped.

27. I take prayer requests very seriously and pray for others until God answers.

28. I enjoy visiting the elderly and sick and bringing them good news and cheer.

29. I am good at planning and following through, especially when helping others.

30. I find satisfaction in doing even small tasks.

31. I enjoy speaking in a way that helps people respond to God.

32. I like to guide others to particular passages in the Bible or to other material that may help them spiritually.

33. I often look for opportunities to share what it means for me to be a Christian.

34. I am good at counseling or giving advice to people who are confused, feeling guilty or struggling in life.

35. I enjoy telling others what it means to be a Christian or about what God has shown me.

36. I feel strongly motivated to give something when an urgent need for money arises in my church or community.

37. When I am asked to pray for others, I feel that my prayers will make a difference.

38. I naturally want to comfort someone who is sick, troubled or worried.

39. I am more comfortable taking instructions from someone in charge than I am giving them.

40. I enjoy helping other people without expecting them to do anything in return.

GIFTS EXPLAINED

The following "Gifts Explained" chart helps you see just how awesome spiritual gifts truly are. As you read the Scriptures, ask yourself:

- What does this passage teach me about each spiritual gift?
- What does God want me to learn through these words?
- How does this verse inspire and motivate me?

Row	Gift	Scripture
A:	PROPHECY—to proclaim the truth or Word of God in a way that brings conviction to the hearers.	Acts 15:32 1 Cor. 13:2 1 Cor. 14:1–3
B:	SHEPHERDING—to have a long-term, personal responsibility for the spiritual welfare of a group of believers.	1 Tim. 3:1–7 John 10:1–18 1 Peter 5:1–3
C:	EVANGELISM—to share the gospel with unbelievers in such a way that men and women become Jesus' disciples and responsible members of the church of Christ.	Acts 8:26–40 Acts 8:5–6

Row	Gift	Scripture
D:	ENCOURAGEMENT—to bring words of comfort, consolation, encouragement and counsel to others so they may feel helped and healed.	Acts 14:22 1 Tim. 4:13
E:	TEACHING—to communicate information relevant to the health and ministry of the church and its members in such a way that others will learn.	Acts 18:24–28 Acts 20:20–21 Ezra 7:10
F:	GIVING—the willingness and ability to help others support and grow the church and the work of God with material resources or money.	Luke 21:1–4 Mark 15:40–41 2 Cor. 8:1–7
G:	INTERCESSION (PRAYER)—to pray for others, identifying with God's will and interest in their lives, on a regular and continuing basis.	James 5:14–16 1 Tim. 2:1–2 Col. 1:9–12 Acts 12:12

Row	Gift	Scripture
H:	MERCY—to feel genuine empathy and compassion for those who suffer physical, mental or emotional problems, and to translate that compassion into cheerfully done deeds that reflect Christ's love and can help alleviate suffering.	Mark 9:41 Acts 16:33–34 Luke 10:33–35 Matt. 25:34–40
I:	ADMINISTRATION—to understand clearly immediate and long-range goals and to devise and carry out effective plans for accomplishing those goals.	1 Cor. 12:28 Acts 6:1–7 Acts 27:11 Luke 14:28–30
J:	SERVICE—to identify the unmet needs involved in a task related to God's work and to do what you can to meet those needs.	Acts 6:1–7 Gal. 6:2,10 2 Tim. 1:16–18

HOW TO USE YOUR "SCORE"

Now look over each of your answers and ask yourself: What did I learn about myself and my own special spiritual gifts? Then take a moment to contemplate what this means to you and consider how you can use this information to better share yourself in Christian service. After all, if you're much too shy to speak in front of a group, you probably won't be a small-group youth leader. What gifts would you rather use—and how? For example, you might instead prefer to put your abilities in typing and filing to use in the church office. Likewise, if you love communicating with other people and seem to have a gift for saying just the right thing at the right time, you would probably enjoy encouraging or shepherding others.

As you grow in your Christian walk, you may wish to come back and retake this survey, just to see if or how you've changed or matured.

Share your gifts with a grateful, willing heart, and you are sure to find a sense of joy and satisfaction in serving others—and serving God. Remember, there are no small gifts when they are God-given and offered up in service to Him. As someone once said, "Your talents are God's gift to you. What you do with them is your gift to God." Amen!

Suggested Readings and Resources

Aranza, Jacob and Josh McDowell. *Making a Love That Lasts: How to Find Love Without Settling for Sex.* Ann Arbor, Mich.: Servant Publications, 1996.

Arterburn, Stephen and Fred Stoeker. *Every Young Man's Battle: Strategies for Victory in the Real World of Sexual Temptation.* New York: Waterbrook Press, 2002.

Beers, V. Gilbert and Ronald A. Beers, general editors. *Touchpoints for Students.* Wheaton, Ill.: Tyndale House Publishers, Inc., 1996, 1999.

The Bible Promise Book. Urichsville, Ohio: Barbour and Company, Inc., 1990.

Dobson, James Dr. *Life on the Edge: A Young Adult's Guide to a Meaningful Future.* Dallas: Word Publishing, 2000.

Doud, Guy. *Stuff You Gotta Know: Straight Talk on Real Life Issues.* St. Louis: Concordia Publishing House, 1993.

Dunn, Sean. *I Want the Cross: Living a Radical Faith.* Grand Rapids, Mich.: Fleming H. Revell Co., 2001.

Fuller, Cheri and Ron Luce. *When Teens Pray.* Sisters, Ore.: Multnomah, 2002.

Graham, Franklin. *Living Beyond the Limits: A Life in Sync with God.* Nashville, Tenn.: Thomas Nelson Publishers, 1998.

———. *Rebel with a Cause.* Nashville, Tenn.: Thomas Nelson Publishers, 1995.

Haas, David. *Prayers Before an Awesome God: The Psalms for Teenagers.* Winona, Minn.: St. Mary's Press, 1998.

Hanegraeff, Hank. *The Prayer of Jesus.* Nashville, Tenn.: W Publishing Group, 2001.

Hunt, Angela Elwell. *Keeping Your Life Together When Your Parents Pull Apart: A Teen's Guide to Surviving Divorce.* iUniverse, 2000.

Johnson, Kevin Walter. *Get God: Make Friends with the King of the Universe.* Minneapolis: Bethany House, 2000.

———. *Does Anybody Know What Planet My Parents Are From?* Minneapolis: Bethany House, 1996.

———. *Can I Be a Christian Without Being Weird?* Minneapolis: Bethany House, 1992.

Lucado, Max. *He Chose You* (adapted from *He Chose the Nails*). Nashville, Tenn.: Thomas Nelson Publishers, 2002.

Luce, Ron. *Extreme Promise Book.* Nashville, Tenn.: J. Countryman Press, 2000.

———. *The Mark of a World Changer.* Nashville, Tenn.: Thomas Nelson Publishers, 1996.

McDowell, Josh and Bill Jones. *The Teenage Q & A Book*. Dallas: Word Publishing, 1990.

McDowell, Josh and Bob Hostetler. *13 Things You Gotta Know to Make It as a Christian*. Nashville, Tenn.: W Publishing Group, 1992.

Myers, Bill. *Just Believe It: Faith in the Real Stuff*. Eugene, Ore.: Harvest House, 2001.

Peterson, Lorraine. *How to Get a Life . . . No Strings Attached: The Power of Grace in a Teen's Life*. Minneapolis: Bethany House, 1997.

Popkin, Michael H., Bettie B. Youngs and Jane M. Healy. *Helping Your Child Succeed in School*. Marietta, Ga.: Active Parenting, 1998.

Shellenberger, Susie. *Help! My Friend's in Trouble! Supporting Your Friends Who Struggle with . . . Family Problems, Sexual Crises, Food Addictions, Self-Esteem, Depression, Grief and Loss*. Ann Arbor, Mich.: Servant Publications, 2000.

Speck, Greg. *Sex: It's Worth Waiting For*. Chicago: Moody Press, 1989.

Stroebel, Lee. *Case for Faith—Student Edition*. Grand Rapids, Mich.: Zondervan, 2002.

Thurman, Debbie. *From Depression to Wholeness: The Anatomy of Healing*. Monroe, Va.: Cedar House Publishers, 1998.

———. *Hold My Heart: A Teen's Journal for Healing and Personal Growth (for Girls)*. Monroe, Va.: Cedar House Publishers, 2002.

———. *Sheer Faith: A Teen's Journey to Godly Growth (for Boys)*. Monroe, Va.: Cedar House Publishers, 2003.

Trujillo, Michelle. *Teens Talkin' Faith.* Deerfield Beach, Fla.: Health Communications, Inc., 2002.

Waggoner, Brittany. *Prayers for When You're Mad, Sad or Just Totally Confused.* Ann Arbor, Mich.: Vine Books, 2002.

Wallace, RaNelle. *The Burning Within.* Grand Rapids, Mich.: Phoenix Society, 1994.

Wilkinson, Bruce. *Secrets of the Vine for Teens.* Sisters, Ore.: Multnomah, 2003.

Youngs, Bettie B. *Safeguarding Your Teenager from the Dragons of Life: A Guide to the Adolescent Years.* Deerfield Beach, Fla.: Health Communications, Inc., 1998.

———. *Taste-Berry Tales: Stories to Lift the Spirit, Fill the Heart and Feed the Soul.* Deerfield Beach, Fla.: Health Communications, Inc., 1999.

———. *A String of Pearls: Inspirational Stories Celebrating the Resiliency of the Human Spirit.* Holbrook, Mass.: Adams Media, 2000.

———. *Gifts of the Heart: Stories That Celebrate Life's Defining Moments.* Deerfield Beach, Fla.: Health Communications, Inc., 1999.

———. *Values from the Heartland.* Deerfield Beach, Fla.: Health Communications, Inc., 1998.

Youngs, Bettie B. and Jennifer Leigh Youngs. *365 Days of Taste-Berry Inspiration for Teens.* Deerfield Beach, Fla.: Health Communications, Inc., 2003.

———. *A Taste-Berry Teen's Guide to Managing the Stress and Pressures of Life.* Deerfield Beach, Fla.: Health Communications, Inc., 2001.

———. *A Taste-Berry Teen's Guide to Setting & Achieving Goals.* Deerfield Beach, Fla.: Health Communications, Inc., 2002.

————. *A Teen's Guide to Living Drug-Free.* Deerfield Beach, Fla.: Health Communications, Inc., 2003.

————. *More Taste Berries for Teens: A Second Collection of Short Stories and Encouragement on Life, Love, Friendship and Tough Issues.* Deerfield Beach, Fla.: Health Communications, Inc., 2000.

————. *Taste Berries for Teens: Inspirational Short Stories on Encouragement on Life, Love, Friendship and Tough Issues.* Deerfield Beach, Fla.: Health Communications, Inc., 1999.

————. *Taste Berries for Teens #3: Inspirational Stories on Life, Love, Friends and the Face in the Mirror.* Deerfield Beach, Fla.: Health Communications, Inc., 2002.

————. *Taste Berries for Teens Journal: My Thoughts on Life, Love and Making a Difference.* Deerfield Beach, Fla.: Health Communications, Inc., 2000.

Youngs, Bettie B., Jennifer Leigh Youngs and Debbie Thurman. *A Teen's Guide to Christian Living.* Deerfield Beach, Fla.: Health Communications, Inc., 2003.

Youngs, Jennifer Leigh. *Feeling Great, Looking Hot & Loving Yourself! Health, Fitness and Beauty for Teens.* Deerfield Beach, Fla.: Health Communications, Inc., 2000.

SUPPORT RESOURCES

Focus Adolescent Services
An information and referral service for families of
troubled teens, *not* a hotline.
877-FOCUS-AS (877-362-8727)
www.focusas.com

AIDS Hotline for Teens
800-234-8336

ALCOHOL AND DRUG ABUSE

National Council on Alcoholism and Drug Dependence
Hope Line (twenty-four hours): 800-622-2255

Al-Anon/Alateen Family Group Headquarters
*(Twelve-step group for family members of alcoholics and teens who are
living with an alcoholic parent.)*
P. O. Box 862, Midtown Station
New York, NY 10018-0862
212-302-7240
800-356-9996 (Literature)
800-344-2666 (Meeting Referral)

Alcoholics Anonymous
(Twelve-step program for alcoholics of all ages.)
World Services, Inc.
475 Riverside Drive
New York, NY 10115
212-870-3400 (Literature)
212-647-1680 (Meeting Referral)

Center for Substance Abuse Treatment
National Drug and Alcohol Treatment Referral Service
(National organization to help you locate treatment programs in your area and throughout the nation.)
800-662-HELP (twenty-four-hour, toll-free service)
800-487-4889 (TDD)
877-767-8432 (Spanish)
www.findtreatment.samhsa.gov

Families Anonymous
(Twelve-step program for family members of chemically dependent people; will provide help for finding places to go, and send free literature and information on their program and other programs that are there to help.)
P. O. Box 35475
Culver City, CA 90231
800-736-9805

National Council on Alcoholism and Drug Dependence (NCADD)
(Offers referrals and information on treatment programs, referring you to your local treatment information center to learn what treatment programs are available in your area.)
20 Exchange Place, Ste. 2902
New York, NY 10005
212-269-7797
800-NCA-CALL
www.ncadd.org

Teen Challenge International USA Headquarters
3728 W. Chestnut Expressway
Springfield, MO 65802
417-862-6969
www.teenchallengeusa.com

CHILD ABUSE, RAPE, SEXUAL ABUSE

Childhelp USA
twenty-four hours: 800-4-A-CHILD

Rape Crisis Center
800-352-7273

Faithful and True Ministries
6542 Regency Lane
Eden Prairie, MN 55344
www.faithfulandtrueministries.com

EATING DISORDERS

American Anorexia and Bulimia Association
165 W. 46th Street, Suite 1108
New York, NY 10036
212-501-8351

National Eating Disorders Association
603 Stewart St., Suite 803
Seattle, WA 98101
206-382-3587
www.NationalEatingDisorders.org

MENTAL HEALTH ISSUES

National Alliance for the Mentally Ill
Colonial Place Three
2107 Wilson Blvd.
Arlington, VA 2201
800-950-NAMI (6264)
www.nami.org
(Check your phone book for local chapters.)

Christian Mental Health Services, Inc.
2180 Pleasant Hill Road, A5-225
Duluth, GA 30096
770-300-9903
www.christianmh.org

MINISTRIES, FAMILY COUNSELING

Focus on the Family
Colorado Springs, CO 80995
719-531-3400
www.family.org
Maintains a national referral network for counselors.

American Association of Christian Counselors
1639 Rustic Village Road
Forest, VA 24551
434-525-9470
www.aacc.net
Also maintains a national referral network for counselors.

PORNOGRAPHY, SEXUAL ADDICTIONS

National Center for On-Line Internet Pornography Usage and Addictions
eBehavior, LLC
P.O. Box 72
Bradford, PA 16701
877-CYBER-DR (292-3737)
www.netaddiction.com

PureIntimacy.org
Developed by Focus on the Family

Porn-Free Ministries
www.porn-free.org

Turning Point
A Ministry of Teen Challenge
See contact information above.

PREGNANCY COUNSELING

Birthright International
777 Coxwell Ave.
Toronto, Ontario M4C 3C6
Canada

Birthright USA
P.O. Box 98363
Atlanta, GA 30359
800-550-4900
Information about abstinence, safe sex, infant care and adoption services.

RUNAWAY, HOMELESS TEENS

National Runaway Hotline (twenty-four hours)
800-621-4000

SUICIDE

Suicide hotline: 800-SUICIDE

About the Authors

Bettie B. Youngs, Ph.D., Ed.D., is a Pulitzer Prize–nominated author of more than thirty books translated into thirty-one languages. She is a former Teacher-of-the-Year, university professor and executive director of Instruction and Professional Development, Inc. A long-acknowledged expert on family and teen issues, Dr. Youngs has frequently appeared on *The Good Morning Show, NBC Nightly News,* CNN and *Oprah. USA Today,* the *Washington Post, Redbook, U.S. News & World Report, Working Woman, Family Circle, Parents Magazine, Woman's Day* and the National Association for Secondary School Principals (NASSP) have all recognized her work. Her acclaimed books include: *Safeguarding Your Teenager from the Dragons of Life; A Teen's Guide to Living Drug-Free;* the Pulitzer Prize–nominated *Gifts of the Heart: Stories That Celebrate Life's Defining Moments;* the award-winning *Values from the Heartland; A Teen's Guide to Christian Living: Practical Answers to Tough Questions About God and Faith;* and the widely popular *Taste Berries for Teens* series co-authored with her daughter, Jennifer. Dr. Youngs is the author of a number of videocassette programs and is the coauthor of the nationally acclaimed *Parents on Board,* a video-based training program to help schools and parents work together to increase student achievement. Dr. Youngs is a member of the Evangelical Lutheran Church and counsels Christian families in crisis.

Jennifer Leigh Youngs is a speaker and workshop presenter for teens and parents nationwide. She is the author of *Feeling Great, Looking Hot & Loving Yourself! Health, Fitness and Beauty for Teens* and coauthor of *Taste Berries for Teens: Inspirational Short Stories and Encouragement on Life, Love, Friendship and Tough Issues; Taste Berries for Teens Journal; More Taste Berries for Teens; A Taste-Berry Teen's Guide to Managing the Stress and Pressures of Life; Taste Berries for Teens #3;* and *A Teen's Guide to Christian Living.* Jennifer is a former Miss Teen California finalist and Rotary International Goodwill Ambassador and Exchange Scholar. She serves on a number of advisory boards for teens and is a Youth Coordinator for Airline Ambassadors, an international organization affiliated with the United Nations that involves youth in programs to build cross-cultural friendships and delivers humanitarian aid to those in need worldwide. Jennifer is a member of the Calvary Lutheran Church and volunteers her time to youth struggling with chemical-dependency issues.

Debbie Thurman, author, journalist and speaker, has been actively involved in many facets of Christian ministry for more than twenty years. She now runs her own ministry, Sheer Faith, in Central Virginia where she leads a weekly support group and works with local and state officials and churches to improve mental-health care and family support. She and husband Russ Thurman have been married for twenty-one years and have two teenage daughters. Debbie is a former Marine Corps public-affairs officer, and is the author of *From Depression to Wholeness: The Anatomy of Healing; Journaling from Depression to Wholeness: A 12-Week Program for Healing; Hold My Heart: A Teen's Journal for Healing and Personal Growth; Sheer Faith: A Teen's Journey to Godly Growth;* and coauthor of *A Teen's Guide to Christian Living.* In addition to her writing and speaking, Debbie mentors teens and families in crisis and works in Christian mental-health advocacy.

To contact Bettie and Jennifer Leigh Youngs, write to:

Youngs, Youngs & Associates
3060 Racetrack View Drive
Del Mar, CA 92014

Web site: *www.tasteberriesforteens.com*

To contact Debbie Thurman, visit her Web site:

www.debbiethurman.com

Wisdom

Guidance

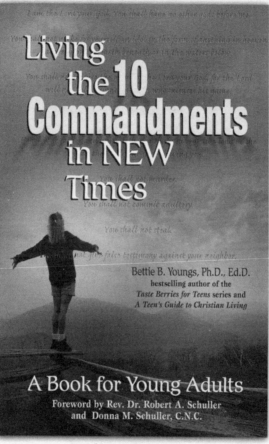

Code #1282 • $12.95

Living the 10 Commandments in New Times will help
you see how God's laws can beam a spotlight on the path to living
a glorious life, one that is pure, strong and victorious.

Inspiration

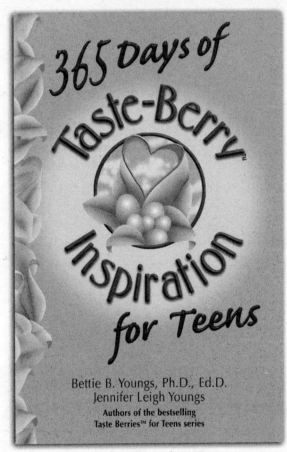

Code #0960 • $12.95

Uplifting, loving, motivating and practical, these
taste-berry thoughts are sure to remind you of your highest ideals and
inspire you to continue claiming them as your own.